ENDORSEME

M000213859

Customer Relationship Imprinting is needed now more than ever. Every business exists to make money and this unique approach to customer service will increase sales and profit at any business! Michael understands the needs/wants of today's consumer and eloquently describes how the business owner can work towards achieving those goals.

—David Farnum
Carl's Jr. franchisee of the year and #1 ranked Carl's Jr. in the U.S.

Michael has helped us unlock our potential with customers! As a result of *Customer Relationship Imprinting* and this partnership, our team now finds more ways to achieve Relational Velcro and make our customer's day.

—Brandon Quaid
Harley Davidson

Everyone thinks of customers in terms of service, satisfaction and loyalty. Those are all byproducts of Customer Relationship Imprinting. Michael Barnett provides a brand new insight to what triggers a customer's loyalty and profitability. This book is customers for life and money in the bank.

—Jeffrey Gitomer
Author of multiple *New York Times* best-selling books, including *Customer Satisfaction is Worthless, Customer Loyalty is Priceless*

As a leader of teams, my role is to sustain the efficiency and reliability of organizational logistics in order to keep the promises made by our sales force. Promises, which over time yield relationships. And for a sales professional, there is no greater asset than the relationships we build. Michael's description of a "Service Architect" hits at the heart of the work leaders throughout an organization do to support this dynamic and integral aspect of business.

—Shilpa Sharda
Roar Beverages Inc.

Customer Relationship Imprinting is a must-have, must-read, and must-implement book for every leader impacting service in an organization. This book will help you remove price from the sales equation and create loyal customers for life. Don't just buy it, bank it!

—Jen Gitomer
Best-selling author of *Sales in a New York Minute*

Kelsey — Keep serving!

CUSTOMER RELATIONSHIP IMPRINTING

THE 6 ELEMENTS THAT ENSURE
EXCEPTIONAL SERVICE WITHOUT EXCEPTION

*To my mom, who spent her entire life serving those around her,
leaving a legacy of kindness and grace that I daily seek to replicate.*

Published and distributed by:

SOUND WISDOM
P.O. Box 310
Shippensburg, PA 17257-0310
717-530-2122

info@soundwisdom.com

www.soundwisdom.com

ISBN 13 TP: 978-1-64095-365-9

ISBN 13 eBook: 978-1-64095-366-6

Author photo by: pictureyourlegacy.com

For Worldwide Distribution, Printed in the U.S.A.

1 2 3 4 5 6 7 8 / 26 25 24 23 22

Thank you

To God: the source of every single good thing in my life.

The Blonde Brigade: Brenda, Roxie and Cheyenne for your unconditional love, support and encouragement as I step into unknown territory. Sharon: for choosing to go on this journey with me and regularly reminding me of my value. Austin, for infusing me with inspiration and helping me to think bigger and reach higher. Jeffrey and Jennifer Gitomer for providing immeasurable writing advice, insight, and knowledge. Dave and the entire team at Sound Wisdom for partnering with me and believing in *Customer Relationship Imprinting.*

THE TOUCH OF
CUSTOMER RELATIONSHIP IMPRINTING
WILL UNLOCK AND ACTIVATE YOUR
CUSTOMER SERVICE IN
A WHOLE NEW WAY

UNLOCKING & ACTIVATING EXCEPTIONAL SERVICE

WHY DON'T MOST BUSINESSES CONSISTENTLY DELIVER EXCEPTIONAL SERVICE?

IMPRINTING UNLOCKS YOUR WORLD EVERY DAY.

Think about the power of your own fingerprint. With your unique digits and today's technology, you can touch your phone, tablet or other device and a small miracle happens.

WITH A SINGLE TOUCH, YOUR IMPRINT UNLOCKS YOUR WORLD.

Your fingerprint also provides you protection. If you were charged with a crime that you didn't commit, the power to absolve you is at your fingertips...literally! However, if you were guilty of the offense, your own prints will also betray you!

DO YOU FEEL LOCKED OUT?

Like staring at a device and not knowing the password, you may feel locked out from exceptional service. It's not that you don't want to get inside. You just can't seem to find the right code to providing world-class customer service and receiving all the benefits that come with it. Your team knows the combination to unlock "acceptable" customer service, but they don't seem to have the right touch to access exceptional service on a consistent basis.

CRACKING THE CUSTOMER SERVICE CODE

Businesses that are providing world-class service have several service practices in common. Chick-fil-A, Nordstrom, Zappos, Starbucks and others seem to have cracked the customer service code. They consistently provide a higher level of customer service than those around them. How do they do this?

JUST AS YOUR DEVICES ARE OPENED BY YOUR TOUCH, CUSTOMER RELATIONSHIP IMPRINTING ACTIVATES YOUR CUSTOMER SERVICE.

Like the various grooves in your fingerprint that unlock your devices every day, the 6 elements in Customer Relationship Imprinting, working together, will activate your customer service in a whole new way. You will not only discover the commonalities shared by organizations that consistently deliver exceptional service, but you will learn how to apply these principles to help your team crack the code to delivering exceptional service without exception.

Customer Relationship Imprinting will not only help you attract, acquire and retain more customers, but it will create an environment where your customers are more compelled to follow you, regardless of any circumstance that comes your way.

Simply put...

FOLLOW THIS FORMULA AND YOUR CUSTOMERS WILL FOLLOW YOU!

YOUR ANSWER TO THE FOLLOWING QUESTION WILL DETERMINE IF YOU CONTINUE TO READ OR CLOSE THIS BOOK!

Can you name a single company whose signature strength is their customer service that has stopped providing this level of service investment because it wasn't worth it?

Neither can I.

It just doesn't happen.

Read on.

If you invest in achieving exceptional service, you will never want to go back to just "good" service. By implementing the 6 elements in Customer Relationship Imprinting, you will attract, acquire and retain more customers than you ever thought possible.

NO, REALLY!

The level of your service will dictate your company's future more than marketing budgets, pricing, convenience, or product/service selection.

YOU MIGHT BE SAYING, "IF THAT'S TRUE... THEN WHY AREN'T MORE BUSINESSES DELIVERING WORLD-CLASS CUSTOMER SERVICE?"

Good question. What do you think the answer is?

DRUM ROLL PLEASE...
THE #1 REASON THAT MOST BUSINESSES DON'T PROVIDE A CONSISTENT WORLD-CLASS CUSTOMER EXPERIENCE IS...

THEY BELIEVE THEY ALREADY HAVE IT!

And why would they work for something they believe they already possess?

Do you believe your company is already providing world-class customer service or just "good" service?

A DIFFICULT TRUTH: MOST ORGANIZATIONS' CUSTOMER SERVICE ISN'T AS GOOD AS THEY THINK IT IS!

This is not meant to be offensive, but it is statistically true.

How good is your service...average, good, or superior?

Often, companies provide moderate to good customer experience with moments of greatness. However, this is not exceptional service.

YOU MAY BE THINKING YOUR SERVICE IS BETTER THAN IT IS.

Don't believe me?

You may want to consider how other organizations respond when asked how good their service is. In fact, a leading business consulting firm did.

AN UNCOMFORTABLE REALITY

Bain & Company, a business consulting firm, recently asked 362 business leaders if their business provided superior service. Not surprisingly, 80% of the businesses said "yes."

THEN THEY ASKED THEIR CUSTOMERS...

After asking these business leaders, the consultants asked 3,000 of these businesses' customers if they, in fact, received superior service from these businesses.

The results were a little different:

ONLY 8% OF THEIR CUSTOMERS SAID THEY RECEIVED SUPERIOR SERVICE.[1]

That's too much of a difference not to recognize that your service may not be as good as you think it is. Maybe your service is as good as you hope it to be, but—

THAT STATISTIC SHOULD REALLY GET YOUR ATTENTION.

As you consider the state of your current customer service efforts, what comes to mind? If you're thinking something like,

"Our customer service is fine…we could improve in some areas, but we don't need to make a bunch of changes,"

there are three words that you need to consider.

THE 3 DEADLIEST WORDS THAT KILL YOUR CUSTOMER SERVICE EFFORTS ARE:

"EVERYTHING IS FINE."

FOR BUSINESSES THAT BELIEVE "EVERYTHING IS FINE," STATISTICS TELL A DIFFERENT, JARRING STORY ABOUT YOUR SERVICE.

91% of customers who are unhappy with a brand will just leave without complaining (**Esteban Kolsky**).[2]
If 9 out of every 10 people leave and don't say a word to you, how do you know what customer service problems you are having?

70% of the customer's journey is dictated by how the customer feels they are being treated (**McKinsey & Company**).[3]
Notice this statistic does not refer to how they are being treated but how they *feel* they are being treated. How do you train your staff to recognize and react to these challenges?

When asking consumers what impacts their level of trust with a company, offering excellent customer service ranked #1 (**Dimensional Research**).[4]
"Excellent customer service," not good service. If you're not delivering excellent service, you're in trouble. What is your business doing to build trust that's based on excellent service?

89% of consumers have switched to doing business with a competitor following a poor customer experience (**Harris Interactive**).[5]
Will your business be on the receiving end of customers who left your competitors, or are they now doing business with someone else because someone at your company failed to recognize their service is not "fine"?

LET ME PUT THIS BLUNTLY:

You don't lose your customers; you lose their business.
Their dollars now belong to your competitors.

THE STAKES ARE HIGH!

Clearly customers are looking for something more and something different. These statistics also scream loudly that customers will leave you to find what they're looking for if you're not providing it!

What are you doing to ensure your customer needs you and they don't get wandering eyes for your competitors?

THE RISK OF LOSING YOUR CUSTOMERS IS TOO GREAT.

Those who don't see the true value of deeply investing in their customer relationships are being left behind...far behind. They think that their decreased sales, lack of customer and employee loyalty, and difficulty developing their business are resulting from something else.

STRATEGIC COMPANIES ARE WINNING.

There are many strategic organizations that have been seeing the dividends flood in from deepening their customer service efforts. At the helm of these businesses are leaders, or Service Architects, who are building brands customers are flocking to and creating a culture where employees are thriving.

NO, THIS IS NOT IDEALISM.

Those organizations that provide consistently exceptional service make more money, see increased market share, enjoy higher customer retention, and employ the happiest team members...from the new hire all the way to the CEO.

" THE #1 REASON
MOST BUSINESSES
DON'T PROVIDE
A CONSISTENT
WORLD-CLASS
CUSTOMER EXPERIENCE IS...
THEY BELIEVE
THEY ALREADY HAVE IT. **"**

Michael Barnett

CUSTOMER RELATIONSHIP IMPRINTING

Leaders who are willing to obsess over making every customer a great customer service story understand the true value and power of customer relationships.

THE FEAR FACTOR

More than an old, disturbing TV show, the "fear factor" plays out in your customer service investment decisions every day.

While many leaders are seeing the increasing value that comes with heavily investing in developing their service, you may be worrying about what can happen if you jump into the deep end of the customer service pool.

INVESTMENT FEARS:

- You fear over-investing your time, money and labor.
- You fear it won't give you the results you hope for.
- You fear lack of buy-in from your leadership and employees.
- You fear the impending wave of new HR issues.

FEAR CAN BE PARALYZING.

It's 3:00 a.m. and "Michelle" steps into an empty Las Vegas elevator. She is nervous about getting into an elevator by herself with so few people around. Michelle feels more than a little vulnerable. The concern of someone following her to her room or sexually assaulting her is a real fear for Michelle. She steps into the elevator alone.

The doors close.

As the elevator begins moving up and she nears her floor, she starts to breathe easier. Suddenly the elevator stops on the fifteenth floor. The door opens to her greatest fear.

It is a tall and intimidating-looking man. He has dark sunglasses, an oversized hat, a bright-colored suit and gold chains.

He looks as if he was just cast as a pimp for an '80s movie. He also has a large Doberman Pinscher with him. Yes, a huge dog.

After standing there for what seems like an eternity, he and his dog step into the elevator.

Michelle is terrified!

As the elevator closes, Michelle gets a sinking feeling deep in her gut.

"Everything is going to be okay" is what she is repeating to herself.

Her heart is pounding.

As the elevator begins to move, the man says something to Michelle that terrifies her. He says slowly...

"Lie down."

Frozen in fear, a lifeless Michelle falls to the dirty elevator floor on her back. She is paralyzed as she looks up at her perpetrator. This was it. No one else was anywhere to be seen.

Suddenly, the elevator door opens, and the man and his dog quietly, but quickly, exit the elevator.

Nothing happens!

She reports the incident to the hotel staff, but she doesn't think they will catch the man who left the elevator so quickly.

That is, until 24 hours later.

THE REST OF THE STORY

The day after the would-be assault, Michelle is checking out of the hotel. She had saved her money for a long time for this trip, but the elevator incident left her ready to pay and head home.

Before Michelle could reach into her purse to take out her credit card, the lady at the front desk hands her the bill for her stay.

To Michelle's surprise, across the front of her hotel bill is written "paid in full" in red.

Michelle is confused.

Who paid for her room?

The hotel employee then pulls from her drawer a small white envelope. With a smile, she hands Michelle the explanation of who is paying for her room...

and why.

Inside the envelope is a single piece of paper. It is a handwritten note.

The note reads:

"THANKS FOR THE BEST LAUGH I'VE HAD IN YEARS... IN THE ELEVATOR, I WAS ASKING THE DOG TO LIE DOWN...NOT YOU.
SINCERELY, LIONEL RICHIE"

Apparently, instead of traveling with security guards, back in the early '90s, Lionel Richie, the multi-Grammy award-winning singer, would dress in disguise and travel with a Doberman in order to move about more freely.

Knowing Michelle would report the elevator mishap, he made the arrangements to cover the costs of Michelle's entire stay.

All of Michelle's fears were unfounded. She feared the worst, but the best was standing two feet in front of her.

Not only did none of her concerns come to pass, but she found herself financially, mentally and emotionally in a much better place than when she was tied to her fear.

STEP INSIDE AND SEE FOR YOURSELF.

In the same way, your fear to invest more in your service is just that... fear. Customer Relationship Imprinting is only a few pages in front of you.

So, step into the service elevator (pun intended) and allow Customer Relationship Imprinting to crack the service code. Free yourself from the fear of investing in your service or the belief that "everything is fine" with all your service efforts.

Your exceptional service will pave the way for greater opportunities to attract, acquire and retain more customers, and it will *pay* your way to seeing increased profit.

However, you need to understand that ensuring exceptional service without exception has to begin somewhere. And that is the 17% Factor!

SO, TURN THE PAGE AND DISCOVER THE NUMBER ONE REASON YOU NEED TO READ, STUDY AND IMPLEMENT THIS BOOK!

ENSURING EXCEPTIONAL SERVICE WITHOUT EXCEPTION BEGINS WITH

THE
17%
FACTOR

CUSTOMER RELATIONSHIP IMPRINTING

THE 17% FACTOR

THE NUMBER ONE REASON YOU NEED TO READ, STUDY AND IMPLEMENT THIS BOOK

ENSURING EXCEPTIONAL SERVICE WITHOUT EXCEPTION BEGINS WITH THE 17% FACTOR.

Right now, as you are reading this, your potential customer is paying someone else a lot more (probably double digits) for the exact product and service they are getting from you.

Why?

Superior service.

That's right.

RECEIVING SUPERIOR SERVICE HAS THIS KIND OF IMPACT.

Someone else has wooed your precious customer away from you by treating them better than you do.

"ACCEPTABLE" OR EXCEPTIONAL SERVICE?

To be clear, most businesses have "acceptable" service. That is, they sell a product or service for a reasonable price and deliver it to customers in a reasonable amount of time.

There is a problem with "acceptable" service.

"ACCEPTABLE" SERVICE PRODUCES UNACCEPTABLE RESULTS.

Every business leader wants to see their business expand and deliver greater profit. However, the payoff they are looking for doesn't come with providing average service. It comes with exceptional service. And exceptional service produces all the benefits that come along with the 17% Factor.

HERE IS THE 17% FACTOR:

AMERICANS WILL PAY 17% MORE TO DO BUSINESS WITH FIRMS WITH GREAT REPUTATIONS WHEN IT COMES TO CUSTOMER SERVICE (AMERICAN EXPRESS).[6]

Reread that again and think about how this could impact your business.

YOUR CUSTOMERS ARE WILLING TO SPEND 17% MORE MONEY WITH YOU WHEN YOUR PRODUCT OR SERVICE IS ACCOMPANIED BY EXCEPTIONAL—NOT "ACCEPTABLE"— SERVICE!

SHEER ECONOMICS SHOULD KEEP YOU READING THIS BOOK!

Where else in your business are you seeing a double-digit increase for selling the exact same product or service you are currently selling? If you can consistently deliver world-class service, then you can consistently see higher margins.

BUSINESSES WILL DO CRAZY THINGS TO INCREASE PROFIT.

If you knew that your customers would pay your business 17% more for your existing product or service, and all you and your executive staff had to do was dye your hair purple on Mondays, what would the result be?

YOUR MONDAY MORNING STAFF MEETING WOULD LOOK LIKE A '90S PUNK ROCK BAND REUNION.

Simply put...you would do it!

There is a big difference between good and excellent service, and it's not just better Yelp reviews or more touchy-feely customers giving you social smiles and hearts.

IT TURNS OUT THAT THE DIFFERENCE BETWEEN GOOD SERVICE AND WORLD-CLASS SERVICE IS POTENTIALLY 17% MORE REVENUE.

Do I have your attention yet?

IMAGINE HAVING A 17% INCREASE IN SALES FOR SELLING THE SAME SERVICE OR PRODUCT AND ONLY CHANGING ONE THING...THE LEVEL OF SERVICE YOU ARE DELIVERING.

THIS IS THE POWER OF THE 17% FACTOR!

Again, excellent service has this kind of power. It is the area of your business that can create the greatest change.

WHICH SIDE OF THE 17% FACTOR ARE YOU CURRENTLY ON?

I guarantee you that the 17% Factor is playing out within your industry right now. It's crucial that your business ends up on the right side of it.

Executing the 6 elements of Customer Relationship Imprinting will ensure that you can deliver exceptional service without exception. It will put you on the right side of the 17% Factor!

BTW: THE 17% FACTOR DOESN'T FIX EVERYTHING ELSE.

Before we get too far, let me clarify something. The 17% Factor won't provide some magical outcome if the quality of what you are selling is poor and no one wants it.

AS A CUSTOMER, YOU DEMONSTRATE THE 17% FACTOR.

Have you ever thought about the fact that Elon Musk, Jeff Bezos, and Mark Zuckerberg are at times...customers?

SO ARE YOU!

For a minute, take off your business hat and put on your customer hat. Not only do you have customers, but you *are* a customer... somewhere.

IN FACT, YOU ARE A PROFESSIONAL CUSTOMER.

You have been a customer almost since birth. As a professional customer, you have no doubt learned to shop for deals! After all, you've been a customer for a long time! Think about your own customer career. You too, as a customer, pay some (not all) companies more money because they provide you with exceptional service, even though you could get the same service or product cheaper, quicker, or more conveniently somewhere else. As a *customer*, you have proven the 17% Factor in the other businesses that you interact with, even if you don't yet believe the 17% Factor applies to your own business.

MOST INDIVIDUALS PRACTICE THE 17% FACTOR!

We all have places where we spend more because we are receiving great service. As a customer, you understand this, but do you see the value for *your* customers enough to invest more substantially in your customer service relationships?

YOU'RE WILLING TO PAY MORE FOR EXCEPTIONAL SERVICE, AND SO ARE YOUR CUSTOMERS.

Are you ready to move beyond "acceptable" service and begin delivering exceptional service without exception?

Unlocking your service, evaluating that your service may not yet be exceptional, believing in the power of world-class service and understanding the 17% Factor establishes a foundation for introducing Customer Relationship Imprinting.

CUSTOMER RELATIONSHIP IMPRINTING: WHAT IS IT, WHY DO YOU NEED IT, AND HOW DO YOU GET IT?

WHAT IS CUSTOMER RELATIONSHIP IMPRINTING?

CUSTOMER RELATIONSHIP IMPRINTING

WHAT IS CUSTOMER RELATIONSHIP IMPRINTING?

ATTRACT, ACQUIRE & RETAIN MORE CUSTOMERS WHO FOLLOW YOU REGARDLESS OF CIRCUMSTANCES

THE TERM "IMPRINTING" IS FAMILIAR TO MOST OF US.

Imprinting has been used in the psychology world for years. Most of the time, when you hear the word "imprinting," you likely think of a baby duckling attaching itself to whatever creature it first sees after being hatched.

However, Customer Relationship Imprinting isn't about first impressions.

It's about developing the ability to imprint so deeply on your customer, through exceptional service, that they choose you...even if they must pay more for your services or products to get you. Customer Relationship Imprinting increases your influence on your customers and builds ferociously loyal patrons even when there are more affordable choices one click away!

YOU HEAR ABOUT CUSTOMER LOYALTY BUT NOT CUSTOMER IMPRINTING!

You have certainly heard of customer loyalty, but you've never heard of customer imprinting. Let's change that!

CUSTOMER RELATIONSHIP IMPRINTING IS MORE THAN A TITLE. IT SHOULD BE THE DESIRED STATE OF YOUR CUSTOMER SERVICE EFFORTS.

I'll start with a definition of Customer Relationship Imprinting so you can understand the impact this can have on your service!

CUSTOMER RELATIONSHIP IMPRINTING IS:

"THE ABILITY TO ATTRACT, ACQUIRE AND RETAIN MORE CUSTOMERS WHO FOLLOW YOU REGARDLESS OF CIRCUMSTANCES"

THIS SHOULD BE YOUR SERVICE GOAL.

Like most any other area of life, you need to develop the ability you wish to prosper in. Athletes, even with natural ability, must develop their ability to be competitive. So do you! You must develop the ability to attract, acquire and retain customers to follow you regardless of circumstances, beyond what you may currently be doing. Finding your competitive edge happens through the development of these abilities.

THE ABILITY TO ATTRACT

Don't leave the attracting of new customers to your marketing or advertising efforts. Your ability to deliver service excellence is some of the most effective marketing and advertising your business can create.

THE ABILITY TO ACQUIRE

Catching customers is a lot like catching a fish. You can attract them and hook them, but the fish isn't caught until it's on the boat. Your service experience is the last five feet of onboarding customers and landing the sale.

THE ABILITY TO RETAIN

Retention comes through intention. There are many factors that go into customer retention. Don't let your average service be one of the reasons that you lose customers. Exceptional service can be *the* reason customers stay with you.

MORE CUSTOMERS FOLLOWING YOU REGARDLESS OF CIRCUMSTANCES

The idea of having customers who follow you regardless of circumstances is the greatest challenge of all. When the economy shifts, customer needs change, your cost of goods increases, the competition rolls in or your staff begin to walk out, you need something that will engage your customers to the point that they stick with you...no matter what!

You must create a need in your customers that substantially increases their interest in following your business through these or any other minefields.

Customer Relationship Imprinting provides you with the tools to accomplish this.

So, the bigger question is not, "What is Customer Relationship Imprinting?" but, "How do I achieve Customer Relationship Imprinting and attract, acquire and retain more customers who follow my business regardless of any circumstance?"

THE ANSWER IS:
CUSTOMER RELATIONSHIP IMPRINTING ELEMENTS!

THERE ARE 6 COMMONALITIES SHARED BY COMPANIES THAT LEAD THE FIELD IN CUSTOMER SERVICE.

Over the last several years, our team at SixSidedService.com has developed a system to help solve the problems facing those pursuing excellent customer service relationships.

We've watched the top companies in the world and have identified 6 distinct commonalities, or elements, that they all possess.

These 6 key practices, called Customer Relationship Imprinting elements, help businesses deliver a higher level of service than their competitors. Period!

THE GOOD NEWS: NONE OF THESE ELEMENTS ARE BEYOND WHAT YOUR COMPANY CAN IMPLEMENT AND EXECUTE.

All 6 elements work in tandem with one another and are collectively needed to achieve Customer Relationship Imprinting.

CUSTOMER RELATIONSHIP IMPRINTING IS

" THE ABILITY TO

ATTRACT
ACQUIRE
& RETAIN

MORE CUSTOMERS

WHO FOLLOW YOU

REGARDLESS

OF CIRCUMSTANCES. "

Michael Barnett

CUSTOMER RELATIONSHIP IMPRINTING

A CUBE HAS SIX SIDES.

To understand the 6 elements, I want you to consider a cube. A cube has six equal sides. If any one of the six sides was missing or weaker than the other five sides, the cube would be compromised. Each side has equal mass and is important to the whole. Think of the 6 Customer Relationship Imprinting elements like the sides of a cube.

ALL 6 ELEMENTS ARE INTEGRAL FOR YOU TO BE ABLE TO DELIVER EXCEPTIONAL SERVICE WITHOUT EXCEPTION AND TO ACHIEVE CUSTOMER RELATIONSHIP IMPRINTING.

Again, all six separate sides, or elements, have equal importance and are needed for the strength of the whole.

If your company is consistently executing all 6 of these elements, you will be delivering "Six-Sided Service." And when you do that, you are achieving Customer Relationship Imprinting: "the ability to attract, acquire and retain more customers who follow you regardless of circumstances."

In order to develop this ability, you first need to leave your transactional flings for customer relationships.

LEAVING TRANSACTIONAL FLINGS FOR CUSTOMER RELATIONSHIPS

Today there is more data about our customers than ever before.

Customers are being given more purchasing opportunities than any previous generation.

We have the quickest and most convenient way in history to deliver goods and services on demand, and yet there is something about the current state of business and customer service that seems hollow.

DESPITE ALL OUR TECHNOLOGICAL ADVANCES AND SERVICE OPPORTUNITIES, IT SEEMS MANY BUSINESSES ARE MISSING...

WELL...

THE CUSTOMER.

While performing the necessary transactions, organizations have been failing to develop a relationship with these customers.

Let me explain.

A transactional fling means that you're providing a service, getting paid, and then moving on to the next transaction. Many people will read this and say, "Yes, this is business." These people are fine with this approach, until they become a casualty of this style of service.

THE TRANSACTIONAL TRAP

Obviously, transactions are important. No transactions equal no sales, and no sales mean no business. But if there is a lack of connectivity with your customers, there will be devastating consequences to customer attraction, acquisition and retention.

Unfortunately, all too often businesses choose to have transactional flings with their customers rather than developing customer relationships, which yields more sales, loyalty and referrals.

In section 1, I will introduce you to Relational Velcro. It is a customer engagement focus to connect you better with customers outside of your transactions.

Consider this question:

WHAT ARE YOU GIVING YOUR CUSTOMER BEYOND THE TRANSACTION?

You may be struggling to answer this question because you may be treating your customer relationships primarily as transactional!

We train people how to treat us!

You may have heard that before about personal relationships, but it is also true in business. You are training your customers how to interact with you.

If it is just transactional, then that's all your customers will expect.

BUT, BEWARE.

When customers view your business only as transactional, they see you as disposable. You are just another business to be compared to your competitors exclusively by price, availability or convenience. It's rough waters for companies that rely solely on always being the cheapest, quickest and most accessible option. There's always a bigger kid on the block. Someone always has more buying power, better logistics or a bigger marketing budget.

I WANT TO CHALLENGE YOU TO DELIVER A LEVEL OF SERVICE THAT MAKES IT EXTREMELY DIFFICULT FOR YOUR CUSTOMERS TO CHOOSE ANYONE ELSE TO DO BUSINESS WITH OTHER THAN YOU!

Remember that connecting your customer with your business is more than just selling them something.

UNLESS YOU ARE DELIVERING SERVICE THROUGH RELATIONSHIPS, YOU WILL BE JUST ONE OF MANY VENDORS TO CHOOSE FROM.

Customers can repeatedly choose your service, but what is there that's keeping them from finding the same service elsewhere?

IT'S ALL ABOUT RELATIONSHIPS.

Achieving Customer Relationship Imprinting begins with developing the "customer" part of your interactions with your customers. Every entrepreneur and CEO worth their salt will tell you that one of their greatest assets is the interpersonal relationships they've developed in business with other leaders, vendors, staff and brand partners.

There are myriads of personal relationship books, dating sites, blogs, couples counseling options, retreats and more to help us navigate the process of developing our interpersonal relationships.

We tend to talk a lot about *relationships*—forming relationships, building relationships, maintaining relationships—*except* when it comes to our customers.

Why is it that when people begin to discuss customers, they quickly abandon the idea of developing a relationship with them?

I'M NOT SUGGESTING THAT YOU TRY TO BECOME BEST FRIENDS WITH YOUR CUSTOMERS, LEARN THEIR FAVORITE COLOR OR PESTER THEM WITH UNWANTED CONTACT, LIKE AN ANNOYING NEIGHBOR LOOKING FOR A NEW BEST FRIEND.

So, what then is the goal of the customer relationship?

LIKE ANY GOOD RELATIONSHIP, IT'S ABOUT CATCHING THEM, PLEASING THEM AND KEEPING THEM!

BEFORE WE JUMP INTO SECTION 1, I WANT YOU TO EVALUATE THE FOLLOWING STATEMENT:

Companies that consistently develop their customer relationships, and not just service, have greater profit; customer growth; customer retention; and happier, more productive employees than their competitors.

If you agree with that statement, this book is for you.

IF YOU DISAGREE WITH THAT STATEMENT, THEN THIS BOOK IS REALLY FOR YOU!

CRI

Customer Relationship Imprinting definition:
"The ability to attract, acquire and retain more customers who follow you regardless of circumstances"

SIX-SIDED SERVICE

The 6 Customer Relationship Imprinting elements working together is collectively known as Six-Sided Service.

CRI ELEMENTS

There are 6 distinct service practices known individually as Customer Relationship Imprinting elements.

'ACCEPTABLE' CUSTOMER SERVICE

Many businesses provide 'acceptable' service. However, delivering this level of customer service does not lead to substantial customer attraction, acquisition and retention.

THE PATH TO
CUSTOMER RELATIONSHIP IMPRINTING

WITH CUSTOMER RELATIONSHIP IMPRINTING, YOU WILL HAVE SOMETHING BEYOND LOYALTY...YOU'LL HAVE IMPRINTING!

"The ability to attract, acquire and retain more customers who follow you regardless of circumstances"

I AM GOING TO INTRODUCE YOU TO THE FIRST OF 6 CUSTOMER RELATIONSHIP IMPRINTING ELEMENTS THAT WILL TRANSFORM YOUR BUSINESS. BUT FIRST, HERE ARE A FEW WAYS TO GET THE MOST OUT OF CUSTOMER RELATIONSHIP IMPRINTING.

STOP! 👆 YOU NEED THIS

FREE ADDITIONAL CONTENT FOR YOU AND YOUR TEAM

Practical Application Points, Group Reading Resources, Exclusive Customer Relationship Imprinting Content, & More

PRACTICAL IMPRESSIONS (PERSONAL APPLICATION CONTENT)

I've created some great tools for practical application of the Customer Relationship Imprinting principles called Practical Impressions.
While there is a key question at the end of each section, make sure you get all the additional free personal application questions and exercises.

GROUP THERAPY (GROUP READING CONTENT)

You should read Customer Relationship Imprinting with your team.
You'll find that the greatest change to your service will come when you read Customer Relationship Imprinting as a group. Use the Group Therapy material at the end of each section, as well as the additional free in-depth group reading content created to help your team thrive. Go to sixsidedservice.com for these additional group exercises and questions.

IMPRINT 👆 ACCESS (EXCLUSIVE IMPRINTING TOOLS)

I've created an exclusive resource for you.
Look for the Imprint 👆 Access icon throughout *Customer Relationship Imprinting*. You will find a wealth of helpful free tools to help you reinforce the strategies in this book, as well as additional exclusive content.

Text me directly at: **949.577.8397** and I will not only respond to you, but you'll become a part of my exclusive Imprint Access community. Being part of this group gives you access to free CRI content, exclusive offers, discounts and more!

FIND A WAY TO MAKE YOUR CUSTOMER'S DAY

1

2

3

4

5

6

CUSTOMER RELATIONSHIP IMPRINTING

The ability to attract, acquire and retain more customers who follow you regardless of circumstances

RELATIONAL

FIND A WAY TO MAKE THEIR DAY...AND MAKE IT STICK

VELCRO

CUSTOMER RELATIONSHIP IMPRINTING

ELEMENT NUMBER ONE

RELATIONAL VELCRO

FIND A WAY TO MAKE THEIR DAY...AND MAKE IT STICK!

CUSTOMER RELATIONSHIP IMPRINTING ELEMENT #1: FIND A WAY TO MAKE THEIR DAY

THEY FOUND A WAY.

A rich businessman finally purchased his ultimate dream car. He now had in his possession a brand-new Lamborghini. It was the jewel of his success. It was his status symbol signifying that he had "arrived" on some sort of financial plane for others to acknowledge.

The car meant the world to him. He decided to take his shiny new expensive red and black toy on a trip to the Alps. However, on his way up the winding, steep road, he began to hear a loud knocking behind him. It was his engine. Once he reached the five-star property at the top of the Alps, he called the Lamborghini dealer that had just sold him his dream car. He told the salesman that the car he was sold sounded like the engine was failing.

The voice on the other end of the phone asked him to leave his car keys with the front desk, go to bed, and not worry about the issue with the car. "We will see what we can do," said the voice on the dealership's end of the line.

Going to bed, the man hoped that the dealer might be able to provide him with a rental for the duration of his stay, so he went to sleep with little worry.

Lamborghini immediately flew two of their finest mechanics to the Alps.

They weren't interested in providing a rental. They were going to replace the engine...in a single night. A job that normally took days was finished in less than eight hours.

The hotel employees watched in awe and wonder as the two Lamborghini mechanics extracted the old engine and inserted the brand-new one in record time. The keys were returned to the front desk with no note from the mechanics. They vanished by dawn!

THEY TUNED AND TWEAKED UNTIL JUST BEFORE SUNRISE, ONLY TO DISAPPEAR AS QUICKLY AS THEY CAME.

In the morning, the Lamborghini owner went down to the lobby. The hotel staff told him that the two mechanics worked through the night to replace his engine.

After hearing of this unexpected and unconventional response from Lamborghini, the man decided to call the dealership to find out what was really going on.

He asked his salesman, "What do I owe for all this work you did in replacing my engine overnight?"

Although he was speaking with the same man to whom he had pleaded his case the day before, the voice on the other end of the line said,

"I AM SORRY SIR, BUT WE HAVE NO RECORD OF THERE BEING A PROBLEM WITH YOUR ENGINE, OR ANY LAMBORGHINI ENGINE...AS LAMBORGHINI IS THE FINEST AUTOMOBILE IN THE WORLD. HAVE A GOOD DAY."

THEY FOUND A WAY TO MAKE HIS DAY!

I am sure the customer with the Lamborghini would be telling this story for the rest of his life to anyone who would listen.

THERE ARE AT LEAST FOUR REASONS YOU WILL ALSO TELL THE LAMBORGHINI STORY:

1. This level of service is so rare it demands your attention.

2. You want your customers to tell service stories like this about your business.

3. You instinctually know that people are always longing for someone to make their day...to be kind to them...or to go above and beyond what they expect.

4. You can appreciate the amount of effort taken to serve this customer.

ALTHOUGH THIS STORY IS AN EXTREME EXAMPLE, IT DOES HELP US BEGIN TO ASK SOME OF THE RIGHT QUESTIONS:

What stories can your customers share about your service?

What have you done to give them a story to tell?

How are you making your customer's day?

The Lamborghini rep didn't ask his customer for a testimonial or tell him, "Don't forget to tell your friends what we did for you!" He also didn't need to ask him to remain loyal to the Lamborghini brand.

THESE REQUESTS WEREN'T NEEDED.

Why?

BECAUSE...RELATIONAL VELCRO HAS A WAY OF CONNECTING YOUR CUSTOMERS (AND EVERYONE THEY KNOW) TO YOUR BRAND LIKE NOTHING ELSE.

WHAT IS RELATIONAL VELCRO?

If you've ever looked closely at the two fasteners that make up VELCRO®, you will notice that one piece has hundreds of mini hooks and the other piece has tons of small fibers to be grabbed by the hooks. If you looked at these two pieces of material coming together under a microscope, you'd see these hooks and fibers joining to create a secure bond.

Once these two pieces come together, it takes a lot of effort to separate them.

I want you to think of the relationship between your staff and customers like the two pieces of VELCRO®. Your interactions are the hooks to your customers' fibers.

THE MORE MEANINGFUL YOUR INTERACTIONS ARE WITH CUSTOMERS, THE MORE RELATIONAL VELCRO YOU ARE CREATING.

When your staff—from the janitor to the CEO—find and develop more meaningful customer interaction opportunities, they are creating more Relational Velcro for your business.

As previously stated, you are in the business of developing a partnership through relationship, not just a transaction.

HEALTHY RELATIONSHIPS DEVELOP WHEN THERE ARE ONGOING POSITIVE INTERACTIONS.

The value comes not merely in the quantity of interactions but also in the quality of the interactions.

It's also more impressive to deliver better service consistently than to give over-the-top service occasionally.

RELATIONAL VELCRO CAN TAKE MANY FORMS. IT ISN'T JUST ABOUT PUTTING NEW ENGINES IN LAMBORGHINIS!

Sometimes making a customer's day involves a lot less "wow" and a little more attention. We all enjoy the over-the-top customer service stories, but it is not sustainable to try to "wow" every customer.

Imagine if Lamborghini sent out mechanics every time there was an issue with someone's car! Their business wouldn't survive more than 18 months. Finding a way to make your customer's day is more about your team being diligent and intentional.

Let me say it this way:

THE GREAT SERVICE MYTH IS THAT YOU HAVE TO "WOW" EVERY CUSTOMER. THE TRUTH IS YOU REALLY NEED TO WOO CUSTOMERS EVERY DAY THROUGH CONSISTENTLY BETTER SERVICE.

HERE ARE SOME SMALL (BUT IMPORTANT) WAYS TO INCREASE YOUR RELATIONAL VELCRO:

- Surprise a customer with a personal note thanking them for considering doing business with your company (even if you didn't make the sale).

- Greet customers by name when possible.

- Give customers a small gift of gratitude (even if their purchase was a small one).

- Serve your customers with a smile.

There are tons of ways to increase your Relational Velcro, which provides the sticking factor for our first Customer Relationship element.

CUSTOMER RELATIONSHIP IMPRINTING ELEMENT #1

FIND A WAY TO MAKE THEIR DAY

Finding a way to make your customer's day is not only Customer Relationship Imprinting element #1, but it is one of the main goals of the other five elements.

While it seems like an obvious goal, you would be surprised to know how many organizations focus so hard on making the sale that they miss making the customer's day in the process.

As you discover the 6 CRI elements, remember that each element is vital to the strength of the whole. Remember the cube! There's a good reason that "Find a Way to Make Their Day" is the first CRI element to discuss. You and your staff must look for ways that you can overdeliver to your customers on a consistent basis—or your competitors will!

"FIND A WAY TO MAKE THEIR DAY!" THIS PHRASE IS SO SIMPLE...

but few businesses are even thinking in these terms. Sure, you hear organizations talking about keeping the customer happy, showing a few videos on customer service to employees from time to time, or answering emails and posts from unhappy customers, but they do not collectively approach their customers with the intention of making their day. Unfortunately, some businesses are fine with delivering mediocre or average customer experiences. They would never say this.

BUT CONVINCING THEM OTHERWISE WOULD BE LIKE TRYING TO WAKE A PERSON WHO'S FAKING BEING ASLEEP.

You must want to be awoken to the level of service you currently have.

Maybe your business, if you're honest, really needs to step up its intentionality about developing this unifying message of making a customer's day among your employees.

The phrase "Find a way to make their day" was chosen very carefully.

"FIND A WAY" MEANS YOU ARE ACTIVELY SEARCHING.

IMAGINE...

What would your business look like if daily, customer by customer, you made their day?

Imagine if in your call center, frontline employees and managers were hyper-focused on finding a way to make their customer's day with each interaction!

STOP AND THINK...

How transformational would your business be if even a third of your employees really had this mindset on a regular basis?

How would this affect your bottom line?

How would your customer expectations change?

Would your employee relationships look any different?

WHATEVER YOUR BUSINESS SELLS, YOU MUST MAKE YOUR CUSTOMER'S DAY. THE REAL QUESTION IS, DO YOU KNOW HOW?

You must know this in order to begin to deliver the service they deserve.

First, what is the definition of "world-class customer service"?

OUR DEFINITION OF WORLD-CLASS CUSTOMER SERVICE:

"World-class customer service is: Consistent service that exceeds a customer's expectations and elevates their experience by thoughtfully fulfilling their stated and unspoken wishes in a way that is superior to the vast majority of similar businesses."

Can your service consistently be described this way?

Most businesses can give examples of when they provided customer service that matches this definition.

However, the first word in this definition is the word "consistent." This is what makes providing world-class customer service difficult.

Would you agree?

Anyone can be good from time to time.

As the old saying goes,

"EVEN A BROKEN CLOCK IS RIGHT TWICE A DAY."

Consistency is what trips up most businesses.

In order to be consistent, you must be intentional and have systems in place to ensure you are delivering the definition of world-class service to each and every customer. This also takes a commitment to providing resources, focus and obsession.

Just like a world-class athlete doesn't become world class by accident, neither do businesses provide world-class customer service by happenstance. More on this later.

HEAR THIS VERY CLEARLY: YOU MUST OBSESS ABOUT ONE THING— FINDING A WAY TO MAKE YOUR CUSTOMER'S DAY!

If you find a way to create impactful experiences by delivering consistent, habitual, world-class service, you are one step closer to achieving the Customer Relationship Imprinting that will transform all that you do.

What permissions have you given your staff when it comes to exceeding your customer's expectations?

DO THEY GO THE EXTRA MILE OR JUST WASTE EXTRA MINUTES NOT SOLVING CUSTOMER PROBLEMS?

Many times, frontline workers, through no fault of their own, follow policies and get a manager when someone doesn't like a stated policy. Most businesses rely heavily on managers to "take it from here." However, those who obsess about making their customer's day have engaged all their staff to deliver the level of service that is usually attributed to those getting paid to care more about and handle more of the problems. Trust, training and empowerment (with limits) will help your frontline staff deliver a better customer experience. It will also help alleviate pressure on management. Too often, managers must abandon their higher-priority tasks in order to help their frontline workers when the frontline workers aren't given the permission and training necessary to handle various issues.

CUSTOMER RELATIONSHIP IMPRINTING BEGINS WITH HELPING YOUR STAFF SEE OPPORTUNITIES TO EXCEED A CUSTOMER'S EXPECTATIONS.

Opportunities to turn a regular transaction into a "make-their-day" service experience present themselves every day...*if* your staff is looking for them.

I was recently on the receiving end of an experience like this. It was two days before Valentine's Day. I went into the local supermarket to buy some flowers for my wife and my two daughters. I took a quick look, and they had a small heart-shaped balloon with a stuffed animal—a kitten—that I wanted to get for my wife. They had several, so I decided to come back the next day to make the purchase. I was just running in for an ingredient I needed to make dinner, and I knew I'd be back. You know where this is going.

When I arrived the next day—now one day before Valentine's Day—every man in the city was grabbing their flowers, balloons and stuffed animals. Of course, the kitty was gone. Now, I am embarrassed to say that I didn't just pick something else and call it a day. I found an employee to see if there were any more kitten-balloon combos in the back. This young teenage worker couldn't find one in the back but said she saw one in the floral prep area. She brought me the stuffed prize, but it was glued to a "Happy Birthday" balloon.

At this point, I said my "thanks but no thanks" and headed for the Valentine's mosh pit that had formed in the greeting card section. A few minutes later, the employee brought me the kitty, now glued to a Valentine's balloon. It took her only a few minutes to make my day.

THIS WASN'T A HIGH-DOLLAR PURCHASE AND COULD HAVE EASILY JUST BEEN ANOTHER TRANSACTION.

BUT THIS SMALL GESTURE MADE MY DAY.

Not surprisingly, this teenage employee has been working her way up the ladder at this location. She has gained a great reputation and built this store a better reputation of going the extra mile for the customer.

TO THIS DAY, WHEN I NEED SOMETHING THAT I CAN'T FIND, I LOOK FOR THIS EMPLOYEE FIRST TO HELP ME.

What if all, or at least a majority, of this store's employees were like this one? This is the beginning of making a customer's day. How are YOU making your customer's day?

THE SECOND PART OF MAKING YOUR CUSTOMER'S DAY IS "MAKING IT STICK."

So how do you find a way to make your customer's day and make this type of experience stick?

YOU CAN "MAKE IT STICK" BY:

- Delivering great service quicker
- Anticipating a customer's need before they ask
- Catching errors with their order
- Making an error more than right by overdelivering when you correct it

YOUR SERVICE MUST BECOME A HABIT!

When people dine at a five-star restaurant, they are always greeted, waited on, and shown more courtesies than they deserve. Why? The staff have been trained to make a habit of treating their guests like royalty.

A few years ago, I took my family to BOA Steakhouse in Los Angeles. I found myself taken in by the tableside Caesar salad service, the lobster mashed potatoes, and the constant attention we were given.

For us, it was a special occasion (my daughter's birthday), but to the staff it was just another day at work. They had established a habit of great service.

I SAW THIS LEVEL OF SERVICE AS A GIFT, AS I WASN'T USED TO BEING TREATED SO WELL. BUT TO THE STAFF, THIS LEVEL OF SERVICE WAS NOT A SPECIAL GIFT—IT WAS A REGULAR HABIT.

Every business right now is training their customers on what to expect regardless of whether the interactions are digital, virtual or in person. Eventually, your customers will see your level of service as your habit and not just a gift.

TOO OFTEN, GREAT SERVICE IS SEEN AS A GIFT AND NOT A HABIT.

One way we can find a way to make our customer's day is to make great service a habit and not a gift. Making a customer's day means that you need to create habits to ensure you consistently provide the best service experience possible and build the strongest customer relationships.

WHAT POSITIVE SERVICE HABITS HAVE YOUR EMPLOYEES FORMED WITH YOUR CUSTOMERS?

Beyond smiles, greetings and "thank yous," what can your patrons expect—specifically—when they interact with any of your staff? By that I mean, what is your staff consistently doing that creates anticipation and higher expectations from your customers?

If great service should be a habit, then there are practices you need to engage in regularly to establish new habits that will draw the results in the direction you want to go.

GIFTS ARE GREAT, BUT HABITUAL EXCEPTIONAL SERVICE IS BETTER! HERE ARE SOME BENEFITS:

#1 | INCREASES CUSTOMER APPRECIATION
Who doesn't want that?

#2 | MULTIPLIES CUSTOMER FREQUENCY
You're building habits with your customer.

#3 | DEVELOPS NEW CUSTOMER EXPECTATIONS
You're increasing the anticipation of your customer.

DELIVERING THE EXPECTED SERVICE

While a fine dining experience is focused on delivering personalized and constant attention, you receive a different type of customer service at a professional baseball game or concert when you go to the local stadium.

This is not a suggestion that your local stadium deliver the same one-on-one attention as the steakhouse. The sheer customer-to-employee ratio destroys this notion, and for many other reasons this is unrealistic and unnecessary. Plus, you don't want the same experience.

When you are ordering hot dogs at a stadium, you expect an entirely different experience than at a steakhouse. Although the prices of those hot dogs are close to five-star dining prices, you have been trained to order, pay and step away.

THE STADIUM FOOD VENDOR MANAGERS HAVE ALSO TRAINED THEIR STAFF AND CUSTOMERS ON WHAT TO EXPECT.

Keep in mind, both the fine dining restaurants and the local stadium are delivering customer service in a way that both their employees and customers agree to. It's an informal contract.

YOU EXPECT THESE TWO EXPERIENCES TO BE DIFFERENT.

You could argue that the stadium service is just as good as that of the five-star fine dining establishment.

Why?

Because they are both delivering the expected experience.

" TOO OFTEN GREAT SERVICE IS SEEN AS A GIFT AND NOT A HABIT. "

Michael Barnett

CUSTOMER RELATIONSHIP IMPRINTING

THERE IS SOMETHING ELSE THAT IS FAR BETTER THAN EXPECTED SERVICE...EVEN GOOD SERVICE. IT'S DISRUPTION!

While your business needs to deliver great service so regularly that it is a habit, disruption is service gold!

Often when we discuss the CRI elements, people tend to think of how they can make a customer's day within the current experience.

WHILE THIS IS A GREAT START...THERE IS MUCH MORE!

Finding a way to make your customer's day by positively disrupting their expectations is what separates the great customer-focused businesses from the average ones. If you can find a way to make your customer's day by moving from expectations, habits, and gifts to disruption...then you really have something!

DISRUPTION MEANS LOOKING AT YOUR SERVICE DIFFERENTLY.

If you drove by George's Shell station in Fontana, California, on the surface it looks like every other station in the country. While they do provide mechanical services—tune-ups, smog checks, etc.—like most every service station, unlike the other stations they saw two opportunities to positively disrupt their customer experience.

THESE DISRUPTIONS TRANSFORMED THEIR BUSINESS.

They have received numerous awards and occasioned a significant revenue increase that can be traced back to these two small changes.

HOW DID THEY DISRUPT THEIR CUSTOMERS' EXPECTATIONS?

If you've lived on the planet for more than a few years, you know that using a public bathroom can be dicey. Using a gas station bathroom is at the bottom of that list—it's to be used only in serious emergencies.

I spent my younger days touring the country with a rock band, and I can tell you, the poor quality of gas station bathrooms is consistent across these great United States!

GEORGE'S SHELL STATION MADE TWO SIGNIFICANT CHANGES THAT DISRUPTED THEIR CUSTOMERS' EXPECTED SERVICE.

CHANGE #1: THEY REMODELED THEIR BATHROOM.

Now before you say, "What's the big deal?" let me explain.

This updated bathroom could rival your favorite luxury day spa!

It is so unexpected that regular customers tell new customers, "Check out the bathroom," often receiving back a confused and bewildered "Okay...sure..." response from the newbies.

CHANGE #2: THEY HIRED FEMALE SERVICE ADVISORS.

The management noticed they had a significant lack of female customers. Why weren't females getting the work done on their car at their station? Most repair shops are run by men who are often dirty, sweaty, and unaware of how to speak to women about many things, including car care.

So, they did something that other stations didn't do.

They adapted to exactly what the customer wanted without the customer telling them. Ladies know that if they go to this repair station rather than the one across the street, they likely will be speaking with another woman regarding their car. And in the automotive space, this matters.

THESE SMALL CHANGES MADE A DIFFERENCE.

George's elevated their service in areas that seem unrelated to increased profits, but this innovation and adaptability in their customer service approach have helped them make the customer's day. This is an example of world-class customer service on a small scale. Their costs to update a bathroom and hire staff were miniscule. With this small change, they elevated their customer's experience.

They welcome comparisons to other service stations.

WHEN YOUR CUSTOMERS BEGIN TO COMPARE YOUR DISRUPTION TO YOUR COMPETITORS'...YOU WIN!

Do you welcome comparisons to your competitors or do you get concerned when someone looks at the differences between you and your competition?

One of the residual effects of hiring female service advisors is that they have been getting a new perspective on their male-dominated business, and it's paying off.

One of their female service advisors just received the Shell Service Champion Award from Shell Marketing.

SHE SHARES THIS HONOR WITH ONLY THREE OTHER PEOPLE ON THE PLANET, AND SHE'S THE ONLY PERSON IN THE UNITED STATES TO RECEIVE THIS AWARD!

Did I mention that disruption is service gold?

A FEW WELL-KNOWN EXAMPLES OF BUSINESSES THAT HAVE DOMINATED THEIR SPACE THROUGH DISRUPTION INCLUDE...

AIRBNB:

Three men disrupted a $500 billion hotel industry. In less than a decade, Airbnb has a $30 billion valuation and is the largest accommodations provider in the world.

UBER & LYFT:

Both app-based driving companies have transformed the way people travel. The disruption has been so great that the government has stepped in to change the legality of the way these companies have disrupted their space.

STARBUCKS:

Are you old enough to remember when coffee came in a red can? Coffee was often only pulled out when company came to the house. Starbucks single-handedly disrupted American (and world) culture when it comes to coffee.

All four of these companies, through disruption, have been able to dominate their respective industries.

Your company's ability to disrupt the status quo could be the missing component to give your business a competitive edge.

What in your industry needs disruption?

Consider a few benefits that will come with your disruption.

BENEFITS FROM DISRUPTING YOUR CUSTOMER'S EXPERIENCE:

#1 | HAPPIER CUSTOMERS

Increasing your considerations and anticipating spoken and unspoken requests are a nice surprise that will put more smiles on your customers' faces.

#2 | FREE PUBLICITY

The more positive disruption, the less you'll have to encourage referrals.

#3 | EMPLOYEE COMPLIMENTS FROM CUSTOMERS

Find a way to make your customers' day, and customers will help make your employees' day.

#4 | FRUSTRATED COMPETITORS

Because they aren't doing what you're doing. You're attracting, acquiring and retaining their customers.

THINK OF DISRUPTION AS THE X FACTOR.

It's that extra something special that makes people choose you again and again to provide the products or services they need.

HOW CAN YOU DISRUPT—NOT TWEAK, BUT SUBSTANTIALLY, POSITIVELY DISRUPT—YOUR CUSTOMERS' EXPECTATIONS?

What are some adjustments your business can make to create a tipping point for customers to choose you more regularly, spend more money with you and share their experience with their friends?

OUR FIRST CUSTOMER RELATIONSHIP IMPRINTING ELEMENT, "FIND A WAY TO MAKE THE CUSTOMER'S DAY," IS A GREAT START. IT'S ALSO AN OBVIOUS ONE.

Finding a way to make your customer's day should be at the heart of all your service efforts. Actively looking for ways to make their day and making the experiences stick using Relational Velcro are vital to this first Customer Relationship Imprinting element.

As you turn your gifts of service into regular habits, you will not only elevate the expectations of your customers for great service, but you will engage your staff to discover the service disruption gold that is waiting to be found.

In the next section, you will add to "Find a Way to Make Their Day," the element that every business consistently delivering exceptional service has firmly in place, by engaging and empowering Service Architects.

SO, PUT ON YOUR HARD HAT AND BE READY TO ENTER THE SERVICE CONSTRUCTION SITE. PREPARE YOURSELF TO SEE BEYOND THE REBAR AND BEGIN TO BUILD UNSHAKABLE SERVICE.

SECTION ONE:
PRACTICAL APPLICATION

FIND A WAY
TO MAKE YOUR
CUSTOMER'S DAY

CRI LEXICON
Key words or phrases from this section

"FIND A WAY TO MAKE THEIR DAY" - RELATIONAL VELCRO - "SERVICE MUST BECOME A HABIT" - "DISRUPTION IS SERVICE GOLD"

PRACTICAL IMPRESSIONS
Practical questions & exercises from this section for personal application

#1 CREATE A LIST OF CURRENT AND POTENTIAL WAYS YOUR FRONTLINE STAFF CAN INCREASE THEIR RELATIONAL VELCRO. PICK 2-3 ITEMS FROM THE LIST TO FOCUS ON THIS MONTH. THEN ADD MORE NEXT MONTH.

Go to: SixSidedService.com for 9 more questions/exercises from section one.

GROUP THERAPY SESSION
For group reading, team building and group discussion

#1 AS A GROUP, CREATE A LIST OF WAYS EACH AREA OF YOUR BUSINESS CAN "FIND A WAY TO MAKE YOUR CUSTOMER'S DAY." ASK ALL YOUR STAFF TO EMAIL/SHARE SUCCESS STORIES OR MISSED OPPORTUNITIES.

Go to: SixSidedService.com for 9 more group questions/exercises from section one.

IMPRINT ACCESS
Get more imprinting tools & exclusive content

Text me directly at: **949.577.8397** and I will not only respond to you, but you'll become a part of my exclusive Imprint Access community. Being part of this group gives you access to free CRI content, exclusive offers, discounts and more!

RIP THIS PAGE OUT OF THIS BOOK RIGHT NOW

AND GIVE IT TO SOMEONE AS AN INVITATION TO JOIN US IN THIS CUSTOMER SERVICE CONVERSATION.

Hello:_____,

This is:_____

I've given you this because **exceptional service without exception is something worth talking about!** I am reading something that I think would interest you!

WILL YOU JOIN ME IN A CONVERSATION?

I started reading this book called *Customer Relationship Imprinting,* and I think you would appreciate what is being discussed, so I want you to join me in reading this book.

Did you know this was true?

56% of people around the world have stopped doing business with a company because of a poor customer service experience (Microsoft).

91% of customers who are unhappy with a brand will just leave without complaining (Kolsky).

A 5% increase in customer retention can produce 25% more profit (Bain & Company).

Attracting a new customer is 6–7 times more expensive than retaining a current one (Kolsky).

One-third of consumers say they would consider switching companies after just one instance of bad customer service (American Express).

I can't ignore these stats! Can you? What are the implications to our business if we are on the negative side of these realities?

This makes me think that if customer service is the difference-maker, what am I doing about it?

Companies that are delivering this higher level of service and building healthier customer relationships often experience fierce customer loyalty and a higher level of retention and satisfaction.

Interested in joining the conversation?

How can you achieve this type of customer service depth that attracts, acquires and retains more customers?
There are some intentional, pragmatic and necessary practices that I want to explore with you that organizations delivering excellent service share.

Join me in reading *Customer Relationship Imprinting*. I want you to read this book because this type of service builds ferociously loyal patrons even when there are more affordable choices one click away!

SERVICE

SEEING BEYOND THE REBAR TO BUILD UNSHAKABLE SERVICE

ARCHITECTS

CUSTOMER RELATIONSHIP IMPRINTING
ELEMENT NUMBER TWO

SERVICE ARCHITECTS

SEEING BEYOND THE REBAR TO BUILD UNSHAKABLE SERVICE

 ### CUSTOMER RELATIONSHIP IMPRINTING ELEMENT #2: ENLIST & EMPOWER SERVICE ARCHITECTS

LEADERSHIP IS EVERYTHING.

There's an old saying worth repeating as we begin this section:

"HE THAT THINKETH HE LEADETH AND NO ONE FOLLOWS, ONLY GOETH FOR A WALK!"

LEADERSHIP MEANS YOU HAVE PEOPLE FOLLOWING YOU.

Your team will follow leadership that also demonstrates service.

Before your employees can "make your customer's day," they will need solid and affirming service leadership. You will need to create and orchestrate a service vision that demonstrates exceptional service through exceptional leadership.

YOUR TEAM WILL FOLLOW THIS TYPE OF LEADERSHIP.

For this section, you will need to put on your hard hat and think like an architect, or more specifically, a Service Architect. Let's go to the construction site and begin!

SEEING BEYOND THE REBAR

To most people, construction sites look a bit confusing. Thin, cheap wooden stakes poking above various elevations of orange spray-painted dirt and mountains of supply piles and concrete slabs outlining the inevitable future can look chaotic to the untrained eye.

Even with workers milling about, it's easy to think, "What are they building?" It takes passing by the construction site several times over the course of weeks or months to be able to understand what is being built.

Have you ever had that experience?

AN ARCHITECT, ON THE OTHER HAND, SEES A PROJECT IN REVERSE.

Architects have the luxury of seeing the finished product before one shovel of dirt is moved. When they arrive on the construction site, they can see what will be.

THEY SEE WHAT IS INVISIBLE TO MOST EVERYONE ELSE.

In all fairness, it's hard for you to see the future of your company's immensely improved service when your own service drive-by experiences don't give a clear picture of what you *could* be building.

As with this construction site, most people don't know what exceptional customer service can look like without someone giving them a clear picture. Even then, people often only see what is in front of them and not what is potentially in their future.

SERVICE ARCHITECTS SEE BEYOND THE REBAR.

Several years ago, an ambitious 50-something entrepreneur found himself sitting at the desks of multiple bankers with artistic renderings of his new construction project in hand, pitching his dream for their investment.

There was a problem.

They could see only acres of dirt, half-built structures, wasted labor hours, and ultimately, they passed on the investment opportunity.

Every last one of them said, "No!" They didn't get it.

NONE OF THEM HAD THE ABILITY TO SEE BEYOND THE REBAR.

With every bank in town turning him down for financing, he borrowed against his own life insurance policy to make payroll for his employees' "wasted labor hours."

HE BET EVERYTHING ON ITS SUCCESS.

Why?

NOT BECAUSE HE WAS FINANCIALLY OBLIGATED, ALTHOUGH HE WAS.

He simply *had* to complete his project. Why?

HE KNEW THAT ONCE PEOPLE SAW WHAT HE CREATED, THEY TOO WOULD SEE THE VALUE.

But for the time being, they couldn't understand what his gift was until they saw the finished work.

WALT DISNEY SAW WHAT OTHERS COULD NOT SEE.

When others looked at the vast building site, they could see only loud, dirty tractors moving dirt from one pile to another. Their view was blocked from seeing any foreseeable financial profit. Some could squint and at least see the building of an amusement park.

Disney saw something more. He didn't see dirt, rebar, lost dollars or even an amusement park.

He saw "the happiest place on earth." He saw what others around him could not. I am sure there is a lot of regret from those who chose not to invest financially in Disneyland. Imagine being one of these bankers' kids and at some point realizing that your dad didn't see the value of Disneyland or believe in Walt Disney's dreams.

WHAT DO YOU SEE WHEN YOU LOOK AT YOUR SERVICE?

It takes some courage to see what the future of your service can look like. As you value creating exceptional service, you will be creating a vision that lifts your staff and customers to see that your business is making strides to provide something better than what you currently have. Others around you may not see it yet, but as you forge forward to build amazing service, others will soon appreciate and resonate with your vision.

Just as Disney saw the value in what he was creating, hopefully you and your leadership will also see the critical need to develop your service and see beyond the rebar.

I want to introduce you to the Customer Relationship Imprinting element that can propel your service efforts exponentially.

CUSTOMER RELATIONSHIP IMPRINTING ELEMENT #2:

 ## ENLIST AND EMPOWER SERVICE ARCHITECTS

Boats, planes, sports teams and even my favorite cereal all have a captain. Captains, although crucial, are not the final authority, but they lead and support the authority of those they represent. The captain of Carnival Cruise Line or Virgin Atlantic Airways is carrying out the wishes of men and women on the other side of their radios. The captain of a sports team is not the final say on who plays on the court or field. There are people higher up in the organization who make the final call.

YOU NEED CAPTAINS TO RUN YOUR SERVICE.

Like a ship or plane, your service needs captains. Without captains leading your team, you will be in trouble.

WE WILL CALL THESE LEADERS SERVICE ARCHITECTS.

In your business, although they are not the frontline foot soldiers you employ, your Service Architects are your officers, directors and managers.

These are the leaders you are trusting to carry out the mission of your service. Behind every business delivering exceptional service is leadership that embraces this Customer Relationship Imprinting element.

IF YOU ARE LOOKING TO BUILD UNSHAKABLE SERVICE, YOU MUST FIRST EMBRACE THIS CRI ELEMENT AND HAVE YOUR LEADERSHIP ANCHORED FIRMLY IN PLACE.

Although Service Architects can be found at numerous levels of your business, ultimately these leaders need to have a direct or indirect influence over the service outcomes of your company.

The leadership structure of your company will determine how the service directives are implemented, but Service Architects lead the charge throughout the various aspects of your organization.

Your company should enlist these leaders and empower them with clear parameters for their tasks in order to develop and execute your service standards.

With the CRI element of enlisting and empowering Service Architects firmly in place, you are creating a blueprint for service success. Service Architects are the engines of your service efforts.

YOU MAY BE THINKING, "GREAT...BUT WHAT EXACTLY IS A SERVICE ARCHITECT?"

I am glad you asked.

A FORMAL DEFINITION, PLEASE:

"SERVICE ARCHITECTS CHAMPION AND LEAD THE SERVICE INITIATIVES BY IMPLEMENTING, DEVELOPING AND EXPANDING YOUR SERVICE CULTURE WITHIN YOUR BUSINESS."

Service Architects should be those who are the most passionate and excited about your service.

They provide the megaphone about service in the corporate meetings and in the frontline foxholes, and they have their pulse on the state of service.

IF YOU ARE READING THIS BOOK, IT IS QUITE LIKELY THAT YOU ARE A SERVICE ARCHITECT IN YOUR ORGANIZATION!

As a Service Architect, you have a responsibility to help others at every level of your organization see beyond the rebar.

IT TAKES THIS TYPE OF LEADERSHIP TO HELP KEEP THE VALUE OF YOUR EXCEPTIONAL SERVICE AT THE FOREFRONT OF CORPORATE DECISIONS AND FRONTLINE EXECUTABLES.

In the previous section, we identified the need to "Find a Way to Make Your Customer's Day."

But you will never get to making your customer's day unless you are able to enlist and empower those around you to lead your staff toward providing exceptional service without exception.

You can have a clear customer communication system where you are hearing the unmet needs of your customers, employees sharing ideas for better service, and CX experts providing you with compelling evidence on how to improve your service.

Without Service Architects enlisted and empowered to hear and respond to these customers, implement your employees' good ideas, or turn the CX expert's evidence into change...you are sunk before you start!

To be clear, a Service Architect is not a defined title at your business, such as CXO (Customer Experience Officer), but it is the name we are giving those leaders who assist in keeping your customer service efforts visible to your staff and customers.

A FEW FUNCTIONS OF A SERVICE ARCHITECT:

- Carry the torch of service by helping to deliver and develop customer service training (procure, adapt and/or develop service training materials and processes as needed)
- Keep CX efforts visible to all staff through communications, internal campaigns and employee service incentives
- Support service efforts by mapping your customers' current and desired experience and help implement needed changes to their experience

These are just a few common tasks that a Service Architect may do. But there are other key factors that make a Service Architect so important to achieving Customer Relationship Imprinting.

SO, WHAT DO SERVICE ARCHITECTS REALLY DO?

SERVICE ARCHITECTS LOOK FOR WINDOWS TO LET MORE LIGHT IN.

As you let more light in, you not only expose some of the dark places in your service that need attention, but you also help your customers see inside your company to view more than just what you're selling.

The old *Field of Dreams* line

"IF YOU BUILD IT, THEY WILL COME"

has been so overused in business presentations and writings that you probably wince at hearing it.

But since I brought it up…

I WILL ADD A TWIST.

What if you already did build it and they did come, but now you're not entirely excited about what you built?

For many businesses, the task of (re)building the structure of service within their current systems seems daunting.

Like the room in which you are currently reading, it's easier to dim the lights and ignore all the dust gathering on the shelves or furniture around you. When the drapes open and the new bulb gets installed, the light reveals what has been hiding.

THE SERVICE ARCHITECT IS LETTING MORE LIGHT IN, NOT TO CRITICIZE, BUT TO REVOLUTIONIZE YOUR SERVICE.

The good news is that it's not time to get out the wrecking ball and level your company's service standards and start over.

HOWEVER, IT MAY BE AN OPPORTUNITY FOR YOUR SERVICE ARCHITECTS TO RETROFIT YOUR ORGANIZATION WITH MORE WINDOWS!

There's a reason that architects added to the modern lexicon the saying

"BACK TO THE DRAWING BOARD."

IT'S NOT TIME TO DESTROY WHAT HAS BEEN BUILT BUT TO REIMAGINE AND REDESIGN WHAT YOU ALREADY HAVE.

Remember, Service Architects look for more windows to let the light in!

In other words,

SERVICE ARCHITECTS FIND WAYS TO DEVELOP AND BUILD CUSTOMER SERVICE INTO THEIR EXISTING STRUCTURE RATHER THAN BULLDOZING THE ENTIRE PROJECT, DEPARTMENT, OR OPPORTUNITY!

"SERVICE ARCHITECTS
LOOK FOR WINDOWS TO
LET MORE LIGHT IN. "

Michael Barnett

CUSTOMER RELATIONSHIP IMPRINTING

HERE ARE A FEW WAYS TO CREATE WINDOWS AND LET THE L.I.G.H.T. IN:

L–LEVERAGE ALL YOUR RESOURCES TO DEVELOP EXCEPTIONAL SERVICE.

- Schedule regular customer service meetings with senior and frontline staff.
- Develop an ambitious budget to increase the finances, labor and time given to customer service training, market studies, customer appreciation and visibility of your service efforts.
- Discover your service DNA:
    D–Declare your deliverables (what is your expertise?).
    N–Navigate and personalize your customer's experience.
    A–Aspire to elevate your service
    (exceed stated and unspoken expectations).

I–INVESTIGATE WHAT NEEDS TO BE CHANGED AND WHAT NEEDS TO BE EXPANDED.

- What practices are hurting our customer service experience?
- What are we doing well in our service that needs to be developed?
- Are there policies or procedures that need to be more customer relationship-centric?
- Are there key players who see the CX vision and need empowerment?
- Are there meeting agendas, memos, and internal communications that need to better reflect and recognize CX values?
- Develop mechanisms within your interactions to recognize personal development within your staff and company.

G–GATHER OTHERS AROUND YOU TO HELP BUILD CUSTOMER RELATIONSHIPS.

- Do you need to schedule one-on-one meetings or group conversations with your staff around a customer relationship emphasis?
- Whom can you employ and connect with to expand your customer relationship influence?
- What adjustments need to be made to employee service expectations?
- Hire a customer experience firm or consultant to give your service efforts more direction.

H–HEIGHTEN YOUR SERVICE CAPACITY AS WELL AS THE SERVICE CAPACITIES OF THOSE AROUND YOU.

- Create your IMS: Imprinting Mission Statement (for internal purposes only). This is similar to a mission statement, but it is specific to your service standards.
- Find great stories and experiences from your staff and celebrate them.
- Send communications regularly to all of your staff about customer service excellence.
- Create virtual or physical field trips for segments of your staff to view other businesses' service and create opportunities for them to give unfettered feedback.
- Read and recommend customer service books, listen to CX podcasts, and/or attend trainings on CX.

T-TRAIN YOUR STAFF REGULARLY USING THE CUSTOMER RELATIONSHIP IMPRINTING METHODS.

- Choose one of the 6 Customer Relationship Imprinting elements each month to focus your training on. (After one year, your staff will have trained on all the CRI elements twice.)
- Show examples within your organization's departments/stores/regions of them executing the CRI elements. Then, reward and incentivize staff based on their service successes.
- Make customer service training part of your corporate culture by writing service training into your quarterly agenda and providing reports on your service to be discussed by the senior staff.

SERVICE ARCHITECTS LEAD WITH A SHOVEL AND NOT A HAMMER.

There is much more to being a Service Architect than being excited about service, assisting the service visibility and letting more light in to see what needs attention.

Vision comes from the top, and there is a hierarchy to the dissemination of tasks, but your staff is watching how you lead. As you "enlist" and "empower," it's helpful to remember that good leadership finds ways to serve rather than to demand.

ULTIMATELY THE NEWS OF HOW A BUSINESS IS LED MAKES ITS WAY TO THE CUSTOMER'S EAR...AND WALLET.

A friend of mine works at one of the largest retail businesses in the world. She shared with me the following true poop story.

Due to my friend's personal connection to those in this true story, and at their request, the company's identity will be concealed.

For most large retailers, it is not uncommon for executives, on occasion, to visit one of their brick-and-mortar retail facilities. It usually consists of speaking with management, as well as walking the facility discussing merchandising, loss and damage, etc.

You've likely seen this happen in a store at which you shop.

YOU CAN'T MISS THIS GROUP.

They are wearing suits and business dresses and stand out like a sore thumb. They move like a cluster and clearly aren't looking to shop but instead to observe.

On one occasion, a few members of the executive team of the previously mentioned company were doing their walk-through when...

SOMETHING STRANGE HAPPENED.

A customer approached one of these senior staff members with her dog on a leash. Extending the leash to this female executive, the customer said,

"MY DOG NEEDS TO POOP."

> **"THE NEWS OF HOW A BUSINESS IS LED MAKES ITS WAY TO THE CUSTOMER'S EAR... AND WALLET. "**

Michael Barnett

CUSTOMER RELATIONSHIP IMPRINTING

The executive said, "I believe there is a small strip of grass outside the store." The customer extended the leash and implied the executive needed to take the leash.

"My dog really needs to poop."

So, the executive, who travels the world in first class, rubs shoulders with the white-collar world, and stays at five-star properties, did something that in her position, she typically would never do.

THE EXECUTIVE TOOK THE DOG LEASH AND PROCEEDED TO TAKE THE DOG OUTSIDE TO TAKE CARE OF BUSINESS.

Once the dog finished his business, he was returned to his owner, who was still shopping in the store. The executive continued her corporate responsibilities without missing a step...or stepping in a mess.

Most executives would have called over an hourly employee from operations to handle this, but this executive understood that leading with a shovel sometimes means scooping up poop.

What do you think this communicated to the various employees watching this unfold? The leadership of this organization was not too high up the ladder to stoop down and clean up after a customer's dog!

THEY SAW THAT THEY WORK FOR A COMPANY THAT VALUES THE SHOVEL OVER THE HAMMER.

These are some of the experiences that help lead people to the imprinting we are trying to develop.

SERVICE ARCHITECTS ARE THE GLUE THAT HELPS THE REST OF YOUR STAFF PLACE A HIGH VALUE ON SERVICE.

Caught or taught? Leading through serving is more effective when it's caught. If your staff see your willingness to serve those under their care, it is transformational to them. It trickles down from the top, ultimately reaching your customers.

Great service begins at the top!

AS A LEADER, OR SERVICE ARCHITECT, YOU ARE IN THE BUSINESS OF BUILDING PEOPLE.

Architects design a great building, but it will take an entire team to realize the vision and move it from the architects' computer screen to concrete and steel.

As you design a customer service vision worth following, it will require a team to execute this vision effectively! People are your investment—they become a legacy that can impact hundreds, thousands, or even millions of lives.

As a Service Architect, you are responsible for the CRI element to build people and watch your service equation begin to produce results like you've not previously seen!

ENLISTING AND EMPOWERING YOUR SERVICE ARCHITECTS IS A PROCESS THAT TAKES TIME.

Rather than revamp or rework your entire company, there should be a clear strategy created for enlisting and empowering your Service Architects.

KEYS TO ENLISTING THE RIGHT TALENT

To enlist: *to secure the support and aid of: employ in advancing an interest* (Merriam-Webster)[7]

Before the decision-maker can "secure the support," there needs to be an understanding of what the goals are. The goals can be best achieved when you have Service Architects who are clear on their mindset, mission, budget and boundaries.

As a Service Architect, or at least the person who will help identify who your Service Architects are, you need to consider some important characteristics and suggestions.

There is no magic number of how many Service Architects your organization should have. Since these are the people championing the pursuit of delivering exceptional service, the more the merrier. However, you will need to provide clear parameters as to what you are enlisting and empowering.

CHARACTERISTICS TO LOOK FOR IN SERVICE ARCHITECTS:

- They recognize service defects.
- They are critical thinkers and problem solvers.
- They are supportive of management/corporate decisions.
- They deliver good service and are committed to improving service standards and practices.
- They are team players and seek to help the team win rather than build their personal statistics.

EMPOWERMENT GUIDELINES:

- Empowerment should be given in small doses.
- Start with empowering them to be encouragers.
- Give opportunities to gather and relay collective feedback on current service systems and standards, company practices, the employee experience, etc.
- Avoid giving titles to your Service Architects.
- Make sure all of your staff understand your service goals.

LIFE LESSONS FROM A BLONDE ICON

I HAVE HAD THE OPPORTUNITY TO WORK WITH TV ACTRESS, AUTHOR, AND ENTREPRENEUR SUZANNE SOMERS.

There are many things that Suzanne has told me over the years that have made me laugh, rethink my opinion, and confirm my convictions.

YOU CAN LEARN A LOT FROM SOMEONE WHO HAS HAD SUCCESSES IN MULTIPLE AREAS OF LIFE.

Suzanne was the larger-than-life blonde bombshell on the TV shows *Three's Company* and *Step by Step*. If you're reading this book and are under the age of 40, ask your parents...they remember Suzanne.

Years later, Suzanne was the brains behind the ThighMaster exercise phenomenon.

" AS A LEADER, OR SERVICE ARCHITECT, YOU ARE IN THE BUSINESS OF BUILDING PEOPLE. "

Michael Barnett

CUSTOMER RELATIONSHIP IMPRINTING

The sales of this device are in the millions! Most recently, Suzanne has authored numerous *New York Times*-bestselling books on health and vitality.

SUZANNE IS A FORCE TO BE RECKONED WITH!

I first met Suzanne and her husband Alan when I was invited to their home for lunch and to hear a business proposition she and Alan had.

THIS MEETING WOULD BE THE BEGINNING OF A LUCRATIVE AND REWARDING PARTNERSHIP LASTING SEVERAL YEARS.

But first, lunch.

Suzanne personally prepared and served the delicious meal. This was a reminder that although she was famous and accomplished in several facets of life, she understood the value of serving other people. Suzanne and Alan were kind, gracious and down to earth.

Our lunch turned into chatting for several hours. Suzanne said two things I remember from that warm day in Palm Springs. Referring to her *Three's Company* TV role, where she played the quintessential ditsy "Chrissy Snow" character that launched her career, Suzanne looked me in the eye and told me,

"IT TAKES A SMART WOMAN TO PLAY A DUMB BLONDE."

I laughed out loud.

In her case, this is very true...which leads me to the second thing I remember Suzanne sharing with me that day. Her second insight is worth bringing up for our purposes. On a more serious note, she said,

"WE ALL HAVE TO ASK OURSELVES WHAT ROLE WE PLAY IN THE DRAMA AROUND US."

Not a bad question for us to ask about our role as Service Architects.

WHAT ROLE DO YOU PERSONALLY PLAY IN BUILDING DEEPER CUSTOMER SERVICE RELATIONSHIPS?

I am not sure what your current title is at your business. You may be the CEO, an officer, board member, entrepreneur, supervisor or new manager.

WHATEVER YOUR TITLE, I HAVE A MORE IMPORTANT QUESTION FOR YOU: WHAT IS YOUR ROLE?

The way we cast ourselves in the story around us at our organization determines the roles in which we cast everyone else around us too!

Regardless of your title, your role is to serve those around you.

YOU MUST ENLIST AND EMPOWER THOSE UNDER YOUR CARE, BUT YOUR DIRECTIVES HAVE THE MOST POWER WHEN DELIVERED FROM A DISPOSITION OF SERVICE RATHER THAN AUTHORITY.

There's more damage than good that can come out of leading from a place of authority rather than a position of service. The way we lead matters. The way we lead in service matters even more.

EMPOWERMENT IN THE WRONG HANDS IS LIKE GIVING A CHAINSAW TO A BABY.

MY OWN "AHA" CUSTOMER SERVICE MOMENT

I had spent several years handling all the marketing efforts for a chain of retail stores, and I was frustrated. While the company was great to work for, the marketing endeavors were a source of ongoing frustration.

To be more precise, another "clever" advertising campaign of mine fell apart at the store level, and I was upset.

If you have been a part of any advertising venture, you have undoubtedly had the experience of your promotion failing at the five-yard line due to errors at the transactional level!

CAN I GET AN "AMEN"?

It's a more common occurrence than most businesses would like to admit. When a marketing team or ad agency has put forth a campaign, effectively communicated details to all the key players, and crossed all the "t's," and still something goes wrong, we look for the cause of the failure. Sometimes a campaign doesn't work because of a poor retail offer, unclear messaging, a bad idea, a lack of perceived value by the customer, or another hundred or so reasons.

At the time, in my mind, the reason this project failed was that the store staff had dropped the ball. Over time it was clear that the store leadership didn't see a lot of value in what the marketing department was doing, and even less in the marketing director (me).

I didn't understand why they didn't care about what I was doing to benefit their stores.

BUT SOON I WOULD FIND OUT.

I am embarrassed to say that my usual process once something fell apart was to retrace my communications with management and draft an email to the district manager proving my innocence as well as their guilt.

I had gotten into a bad habit of blaming and then demanding respect for my various brilliant, or not so brilliant, campaigns.

IN RETROSPECT, THERE WAS PLENTY OF CULPABILITY ON MY END, BUT AT THE TIME I DIDN'T SEE MOST OF IT.

Regardless of why the campaign failed, I needed to look at this situation differently. This would be the beginning of a significant change in my approach to working with others.

> **"WHATEVER YOUR TITLE, I HAVE A MORE IMPORTANT QUESTION FOR YOU: WHAT IS YOUR ROLE?"**

Michael Barnett

CUSTOMER RELATIONSHIP IMPRINTING

SEEING OUR ROLE IN THE DRAMA

I finally saw my role in the drama!

THIS WAS A SERVICE MINDSET-ALTERING EVENT FOR ME.

I missed the opportunity to serve those around me. For several years, I had miscast myself in the starring role.

IT WOULD BE AS STRANGE AS CASTING SYLVESTER STALLONE AS GANDHI.

It was at this point that I realized I needed to see how I could serve the managers, not vice versa.

I MISTAKENLY SAW EVERYONE ELSE AROUND ME AS SUPPORTING ACTORS, ANTAGONISTS, OR EXTRAS TO MY STARRING ROLE.

I had been believing the managers were supposed to serve the marketing initiatives and do what I requested of them. In retrospect, it's clear why many of the managers had little interest in me or my projects.

I miscast myself! How about you?

HOW HAVE YOU CAST YOURSELF IN THE LATEST EPISODE AT YOUR PLACE OF BUSINESS?

This is one of the most important questions of this section:

ARE YOU SEEING YOUR ROLE IN THE BIGGER PICTURE, OR ARE YOU SEEING THE BIG PICTURE NEEDING YOUR ROLE?

What would your relationships with superiors and those under your care look like if you saw your role as a support to help and assist them? In the United States, there is an idea perpetuated that the more "successful" someone becomes, the more they should expect others to serve them.

REGARDLESS OF THE TITLE ON YOUR DOOR OR YOUR EMAIL SIGNATURE, YOUR SERVICE STATUS ELEVATES AS YOU SERVE.

YOUR SERVICE ARCHITECTS PROVIDE THE LIFEBLOOD YOUR TEAM NEEDS TO BUILD UNSHAKABLE SERVICE.

Good leadership is the key to most any success in business. You and your staff have the challenge to help those around you see beyond the rebar. Your Service Architects are the ultimate key to your service success.

REMEMBER: LEADERSHIP IS EVERYTHING.

Leading with a shovel and letting in more light are integral to your service team's ability to provide exceptional service without exception. Finding your service role, regardless of your title, will inspire those you lead to follow you and your commitment to giving every customer the experience they deserve.

Now, as you create your leadership and enlist and empower them, you are setting up your business for incredible success. Success, however, does not come with just having good leadership. There needs to be a willing, capable, and well-equipped team to follow the leadership foundation that you have built.

THIS IS THE BEGINNING OF BUILDING UNSHAKABLE SERVICE!

But what about your frontline employees? Are they ready and able to deliver exceptional service without exception?

MAYBE THEY JUST NEED YOU TO HELP THEM FIND THEIR INTERNAL SERVICE SWITCH!

CRI LEXICON
Key words or phrases from this section

"ENLIST & EMPOWER SERVICE ARCHITECTS" - "SEEING BEYOND THE REBAR" - "SERVICE ARCHITECTS LOOK FOR WINDOWS TO LET MORE LIGHT IN" - "SERVICE ARCHITECTS LEAD WITH A SHOVEL AND NOT A HAMMER" - "WHATEVER YOUR TITLE...WHAT IS YOUR ROLE?"

PRACTICAL IMPRESSIONS
Practical questions & exercises from this section for personal application

#1 WHAT ARE THE TOP 3 CHALLENGES & THE TOP 3 OPPORTUNITIES AT YOUR BUSINESS RIGHT NOW FOR A SERVICE ARCHITECT? COME UP WITH A PLAN TO ADDRESS EACH ONE OF THESE.

Go to: SixSidedService.com for 9 more questions/exercises from section two.

GROUP THERAPY SESSION
For group reading, team building and group discussion

#1 AS A GROUP, WRITE DOWN THE BEST POTENTIAL CUSTOMER COMMENTS YOU COULD EVER GET! THEN, LIKE DISNEY, LOOK BEYOND THE REBAR TO DETERMINE THE STEPS NEEDED TO MAKE THE COMPLIMENTS A REALITY.

Go to: SixSidedService.com for 9 more group questions/exercises from section two.

IMPRINT ACCESS
Get more imprinting tools & exclusive content

Text me directly at: **949.577.8397** and I will not only respond to you, but you'll become a part of my exclusive Imprint Access community. Being part of this group gives you access to free CRI content, exclusive offers, discounts and more!

CUSTOMER RELATIONSHIP IMPRINTING

The ability to attract, acquire and retain more customers who follow you regardless of circumstances

1 FIND A WAY TO MAKE YOUR CUSTOMER'S DAY

2 ENLIST & EMPOWER SERVICE ARCHITECTS

3 DEVELOP CUSTOMER-CENTRIC EMPLOYEES

THE INTERNAL
TURNING ON CUSTOMER-CENTRIC THINKING
SERVICE SWITCH:
WITH YOUR FRONTLINE EMPLOYEES
IS IT OFF OR ON?

CUSTOMER RELATIONSHIP IMPRINTING
ELEMENT NUMBER THREE

THE INTERNAL SERVICE SWITCH: IS IT OFF OR ON?

TURNING ON CUSTOMER-CENTRIC THINKING WITH YOUR FRONTLINE EMPLOYEES

CUSTOMER RELATIONSHIP IMPRINTING ELEMENT #3: DEVELOP CUSTOMER-CENTRIC EMPLOYEES

Take a quick time-out from reading this book.

No really!

Set the book down or close your digital version and try an experiment.

RIGHT NOW, I WANT YOU TO PICK UP YOUR PHONE AND TEXT OR TALK TO TWO OR THREE OF YOUR EMPLOYEES.

Assure your employees that you are just wanting to get their immediate feedback and no answer is a wrong answer.

Ask them this question:

"WHAT IS THE MOST IMPORTANT JOB IN OUR COMPANY?"

Write their answers here:

_____

_____

_____

_____

IF THEY ANSWER, "THE MOST IMPORTANT JOB IN OUR COMPANY IS TO...

"take care of the customer,"

"serve our guests,"

"find a way to make our customer's day,"

or something along these lines, then you are on the right track.

However, if they point to a task, sales goal, staff position, or anything that is not customer-centric as the most important job, then you have work to do.

You will need to provide guidance for your staff to be more customer-centric.

SO, HOW DO YOU HELP YOUR EMPLOYEES KEEP YOUR CUSTOMERS TOP OF MIND?

They can't make their customer's day if they're not even thinking of the customer.

CUSTOMER RELATIONSHIP IMPRINTING ELEMENT #3:

DEVELOP CUSTOMER-CENTRIC EMPLOYEES

For some of your staff, the switch is off...the lights are out, and no one is home. Every business has some employees like this. It is inevitable.

For other employees, their switch is stuck somewhere in between off and on, so they fail to give a consistent level of service. Some days these employees provide great service, and other days...not so much. Customer Relationship Imprinting requires consistency.

Finally, there are others who think differently about their role with the customer. It's as if they have a service switch that is turned "on."

YOU CAN HELP YOUR STAFF BECOME MORE CUSTOMER-CENTRIC BY ENGAGING THEIR INTERNAL SERVICE SWITCH.

What is the Internal Service Switch, and how does it work?

THE INTERNAL SERVICE SWITCH IS:

"The ability to turn on customer-centric thinking."

SINCE BEHAVIOR IS DETERMINED BY BELIEF AND BELIEF IS DETERMINED BY WHAT YOU THINK ABOUT, I WANT YOU TO LOOK AT THE WAY YOUR EMPLOYEES THINK.

Without the Internal Service Switch (I.S.S.) turned on within your employees, there is no way you will achieve Customer Relationship Imprinting. On the other hand, if you can help your staff engage their customer-centric thinking, you are miles ahead of your competition.

This is important!

Correction...

This is paramount!

HOLD ON A MINUTE!

Before you dismiss the Internal Service Switch as just a creative phrase with no practical basis or application in the real world, there is something you should consider.

YOUR MIND COMES PRE-LOADED WITH A SERVICE SWITCH.

Your brain was designed with something called the Reticular Activating System (RAS).

Every second, your brain must process 100 million impulses that strike your brain. Yes...every second! Imagine if, while you're reading this, you had to respond to every piece of stimuli bombarding your senses: ambient sounds, people talking, your own breathing, your skin rubbing against your clothing or the hum of your computer.

If your brain had to respond to all this stimulation, you would quickly go insane. So, at the base of your brain is your God-given filter that directs your brain traffic so you don't have to respond actively to everything in your environment.

"THE INTERNAL SERVICE SWITCH IS:

'THE ABILITY TO TURN ON CUSTOMER-CENTRIC THINKING.' "

Michael Barnett

CUSTOMER RELATIONSHIP IMPRINTING

The RAS is the gatekeeper of your brain.

BETTER YET, THINK OF IT AS YOUR ATTENTION FILTER.

"The reticular activating system filters out repetitive stimuli, preventing sensory overload."[8]

"The Reticular Activating System (RAS) is a bundle of nerves at our brainstem that filters out unnecessary information, so the important stuff gets through.... Your RAS takes what you focus on and creates a filter for it. It then sifts through the data and presents only the pieces that are important to you. All of this happens without you noticing, of course. The RAS programs itself to work in your favor without you actively doing anything."[9]

"The Reticular Activating System (RAS)...filters all incoming stimuli and makes the 'decision' as to what people attend to or ignore. Information constantly comes into the brain from the body's sensory receptors. At any given moment we are experiencing sights, sounds, smells, tastes and tactile input. It is impossible for us to be consciously aware of all this sensory information. Therefore the brain has a filter (the RAS) that selects the sensory information to which we consciously attend."[10]

THERE ARE THREE MAJOR PIECES OF DATA YOUR RETICULAR ACTIVATING SYSTEM PRIORITIZES.

It's not that you can't hear or respond to anything else, but it does mean that these three types of brain impulses, according to science, get put to the front of the line...so to speak. We all have priorities... even our brains.

THE THREE THINGS THE RETICULAR ACTIVATING SYSTEM PRIORITIZES TO GET YOUR ATTENTION ARE:

1. What you value
2. What you fear
3. What is novel (odd or out of the ordinary) to you

1. WHAT YOU VALUE: THE RETICULAR ACTIVATING SYSTEM PRIORITIZES WHAT MATTERS TO YOU

Have you noticed that when you're single and lonely, all you ever seem to see are couples kissing and holding hands? Or if you're in the market for a new home, the same houses that you didn't even notice yesterday when you weren't thinking about moving now seem to jump out everywhere.

The romantic relationships and homes were always there, but you noticed them only after they had become valuable to you. I am not speaking about that ad you clicked on and now is getting retargeted to every other site you visit. Yes, advertisers know a thing or two about your RAS. Advertisers often use taglines based on value. Look at any ad. The advertisements that you are looking at are most likely attempting to tap into something that you value. They do this because it works. We are attracted to what we value.

2. THE SECOND CATEGORY YOUR RAS RESPONDS TO IS WHAT YOU FEAR: THE RAS FILTER ALLOWS WHAT YOU SENSE AS A THREAT TO REACH YOU AS AN ALARM.

If you are in a crowded, noisy room with multiple conversations going on, you are drawn to words you hear that tap into your fear. "Cancer," "terrorist," "gun," and hundreds of other words and images cut through everything else. Why?

Because your brain's filter is looking out for your best interests. It's the survival data that is meant to reach you, so you respond immediately. Politicians and salespeople use fear phrases all the time to get your attention and get past the gates of your Reticular Activating System.

3. THE THIRD CATEGORY OF DATA THAT GETS THROUGH THE RAS FIRST IS INFORMATION YOU DETERMINE AS ODD, NOVEL OR OUT OF THE ORDINARY.

The RAS allows in novel information that doesn't fit into what you experience as ordinary or normal. Social media video titles, images and media headlines are filled with unique and bizarre statements. Out-of-the-ordinary headlines like "three-legged man wins marathon" get our attention because the Reticular Activating System is susceptible to that which is novel.

YOU MAY BE THINKING,

"This is all very nice, but what does the Reticular Activating System have to do with 'Billy,' our new hire, who has poor customer service skills and can't get to work on time or seem to think critically about solving customer problems to save his life?"

THE ANSWER IS...A LOT MORE THAN YOU MAY THINK.

While there are many other factors that motivate your employees, recognizing RAS is a good place for you to start when considering giving your employees better tools to navigate service.

I can't recommend helping your staff navigate service using novelty as a regular training technique. I'm not even sure what that would look like. And using fear to train and motivate your staff may not be the best idea if you want to produce a culture that breeds happy and healthy employees.

So, if you want "Billy" and his co-workers to be more customer-centric and exceed customer expectations, you must develop training prompts or cues to tap into their I.S.S.

LET'S CALL YOUR PROMPTS OR CUES "SERVICE SWITCH TRIGGERS"!

SERVICE SWITCH TRIGGERS

The five Service Switch Triggers are value-based prompts, or cues, to prime your staff to think intentionally about customers and deliver a higher level of service.

INTERNAL SERVICE SWITCH TRIGGER #1
DEVELOP CUSTOMER-CENTRIC EMPLOYEES BY USING VALUES-BASED COMMUNICATION

It is important when leading with values to know what is important to your internal culture. Section 5 will go more in depth on the topic of culture, but you if you're tapping into the I.S.S., you need to know what your staff values and what they don't value.

" THE 3 THINGS THE RETICULAR ACTIVATING SYSTEM PRIORITIZES

TO GET YOUR ATTENTION ARE:

WHAT YOU VALUE, WHAT YOU FEAR &

WHAT IS OUT OF THE ORDINARY.

Michael Barnett

CUSTOMER RELATIONSHIP IMPRINTING

HERE ARE A FEW SUGGESTIONS:

- Survey your employees and ask what type of humanitarian and community sponsorships they think your company should be supporting. Use your survey data to align your employees with various causes that are important to them by providing corporate sponsorship or by creating business campaigns that align with these values.

- When giving employee bonuses, give them the option of comp days, gift cards or money. Some of your employees value time over money. Others feel more appreciated when you give them a gift card to their favorite website, amusement park or restaurant.

- Communicate your service goals to your staff as values and not just policies. Rather than a sign that says, "No personal phone calls on the workroom floor," the sign could read, "We value your privacy. Please take all personal calls off the workroom floor." Same message communicated differently. Subtle but effective in tapping into values and not just rules.

Using value-based communication is worth your time. It will begin to help you to develop customer-centric employees.

INTERNAL SERVICE SWITCH TRIGGER #2
DEVELOP CUSTOMER-CENTRIC EMPLOYEES BY CREATING SERVICE RITUALS

Think of service rituals as the electricity to the Internal Service Switch! Becoming more customer-centric means triggering your Internal Service Switch using these rituals everywhere from the conference room to the workroom.

These regular rituals will help connect everyone at your business to the customer, not just the frontline employees.

WHAT IS A RITUAL?

We will borrow and adopt a service ritual definition from the book *Rituals for Work*:

"Actions that a person or group does repeatedly, following a similar pattern or script in which they've imbued symbolism and meaning."[11]

Helping your staff think about the customer will always be a challenge.

Making connections between employee values and their daily tasks as well as creating rituals to reinforce these values is a good start.

WHAT REGULAR SYMBOLIC RITUALS DO YOU CURRENTLY USE WITH YOUR EMPLOYEES TO HELP THEM STAY FOCUSED ON THE CUSTOMER?

HERE ARE A FEW IDEAS:

- **CREATE A PERPETUAL FIVE-STAR SERVICE TROPHY.** Give the trophy to an employee, department or store with the most five-star reviews at the end of each week, month, or quarter. Make it fun and endow the winners with bragging rights that could include mailing a photo of the winners with their trophy. Each winner is presented the trophy by the previous winner. That way it is your employees giving the award and not corporate.

- **BEGIN EACH MEETING WITH A CX STORY.** In morning team gatherings with frontline employees, district meetings, leadership forums, etc., open with a service story. Make this part of your company's DNA. Each time, assign a different employee to share a story about a customer's positive or negative experience with your business. Sharing the task of finding the story will require employees to look for these stories and encourage them to be thinking in a more customer-centric manner. You will be surprised at all the good (and not-so-good) service that's going on in your organization.

I would recommend creating ground rules that the story can't be something a customer shared on social media or is older that one week. Don't worry if initially your team can't find good customer service stories regularly. Stick with it, and your staff will begin to think more about customers and, as a result, you'll hear more stories. Hopefully the positive customer experience stories will outweigh the negative ones. Use both as teaching and reinforcement opportunities.

- **IMPLEMENT THE SERVICE C.A.R.E. SHEET.** Use the Service C.A.R.E. sheet described in I.S.S. Trigger #5 as a ritual.

Rituals can also be ones that your customers reinforce. The fast-food franchise Arby's has a big manual bell at the exit of every location. Underneath it is a sign that reads: "If your service was great, ring the bell." If you ring the bell, you hear a collective "thank you" from the staff.

This ritual is for both the customers and the employees.

The bell idea may not work if you run a meditation studio! Find some rituals that make sense for your business to trigger the Internal Service Switch.

INTERNAL SERVICE SWITCH TRIGGER #3
DEVELOP CUSTOMER-CENTRIC EMPLOYEES BY PROVIDING T.O.O.L.S.

I want to spend a little more time on Internal Service Switch Trigger #3 because it gives the essential tools needed for your employees' customer service toolbelt. This the baseline of what is needed, but get this right and you will solve 80% of your issues on the front line.

" THE FIVE SERVICE SWITCH TRIGGERS

ARE VALUE-BASED PROMPTS, OR CUES, **TO PRIME YOUR STAFF TO THINK INTENTIONALLY ABOUT CUSTOMERS** AND DELIVER A HIGHER LEVEL **OF SERVICE. "**

Michael Barnett

CUSTOMER RELATIONSHIP IMPRINTING

T = TRAINING

First, you need to spend money on training. If you want to know what is important to a company, look at where the money is spent. It's also true that the money that is cut from a budget communicates what is not as important.

Thirty years ago, American Airlines removed one thing off their in-flight meals in order to save money. They realized that by taking just one olive off each food tray, they could save $40,000 a year.[12]

While this was the right decision for American Airlines, unfortunately many people see customer service training as a garnish.

YOUR BUSINESS HAS DECIDED THAT THE DEDICATION OF RESOURCES TO ACHIEVE CUSTOMER SERVICE IS EITHER A MAIN ENTREE OR A GARNISH!

After reading the above statement, many will try to make themselves feel a little better by saying their company treats customer relationships with more respect than a garnish. Perhaps a side dish?

There are other places in your business to make compromises. Not here.

How important is investing in customer relationships to your business? Budgets don't lie.

Second, you need three types of training to succeed:

GOOD TRAINING, EFFECTIVE TRAINING, AND CONSISTENT TRAINING!

This should be your mantra as you focus on providing world-class customer service and achieving Customer Relationship Imprinting. Developing customer-centric employees requires training.

So many businesses hire a new person, send them though a customer service class or video and then unleash them on their greatest asset (customers) to represent their company.

This is insane!

It is always amazing how little on-site training most businesses give to their employees—mostly frontline and entry-level employees.

They often set their new hires up for failure when they seek to fill a hole and tell them, "We are here if you have any questions," or, "You'll learn as you go." Yes, they likely will learn as they go, but at the expense of how many customers? How many customers have you agitated or lost because of this approach?

LEAVE THE TOP SERVICE TRAINING EXCUSES BEHIND.

TRAINING EXCUSE #1:
"We are short-staffed and just don't have the time."

- Training helps to prevent poor service and customer loss and alleviates pressure on managers.
- There is no greater R.O.I. than employee investment. It not only trains your employees but makes your staff better at training and identifying talent, or lack thereof.

TRAINING EXCUSE #2:

"The job is not that hard, so not a lot of training is required."

- There are reasons that shampoo has instructions printed on the label on how to use the product. Don't assume anything about an employee.
- Observe, evaluate, train and repeat.

TRAINING EXCUSE #3:

"Training costs too much time, money and energy."

- Losing a customer is significantly more expensive than training. Plus, if you have high turnover, then your training should be even more of a priority to be able to hire more efficiently and recognize problems quicker. Also, you will have a lot of practice in training if you have a lot of turnover!

COMMIT TO TRAINING!

In the previous section, you were introduced to Service Architects. Behind every great architect is a coach, mentor, or trainer. Like your personal, relational and business coaching, your customer service coaching needs to be a priority! I want you to consider training your Service Architects. Your Service Architects should have a mentor, either inside or outside your company. Like any good architect, you should be having someone more knowledgeable than you look over your plans and help you through the multiple phases of building your service.

The healthiest people receive counseling when things are going well, not when all the wheels have fallen off. Don't wait for a slew of customer complaints to make their way from social media or Yelp to your CEO, manager, or regional director's device to begin receiving coaching and training.

A LITTLE SHAMELESS PLUG

Bring in a consultant to start your process of delivering exceptional service.

At SixSidedService.com, you can find free and paid training. There are also coaching opportunities. This can help your company in significant ways to coach and develop your team.

You don't need to use my company, but the point is...make the investment in training your Service Architects with qualified CX specialists.

Having a fantastic leadership team is one thing, but providing support to train your staff is an entirely different (and vital) piece of developing exceptional service without exception.

Your team and customers will thank you for it. Plus...Service Architects are worth it!

If you are looking for more free resources to train your team,

GO TO: SIXSIDEDSERVICE.COM/FREE
FOR A FREE COPY OF "THE SERVICE CLARITY COACHING GUIDE."

O = OWNERSHIP OF CUSTOMER SERVICE

If every employee is going to be expected to provide exceptional customer service, then there must be ownership! When we own something, we care about it more than when we borrow, rent, or get for free. Remember how little you cared about the lawn, wall color and plumbing when you rented? How much more important did these things become once you owned your home?

Ownership is a key tool in the belt of your employee, but ownership isn't easy.

A FEW WAYS TO CREATE EMPLOYEE OWNERSHIP:

1. Solicit input on decisions that impact their department.

2. Let employees feel the weight and wing of ownership by giving them responsibilities that require you to trust them more than you have. As a young 20-year-old, I remember receiving the keys to open the shop I had been working at. Although I was just an hourly employee, being given this trust to open the shop gave me a sense of pride, professional growth and ownership. What opportunity can you provide that doesn't require a raise or promotion?

3. Explain some of your company decisions to help employees see the bigger picture.

4. Help employees understand that their role is vital even if it's a small role.

A FEW EXAMPLES:

TO THE JANITOR who says, "I just clean the bathrooms and take out the trash," remind them that if they don't keep the bathroom clean and the trash emptied, a mom of three may come into our location and after seeing a dirty bathroom decide not to return. A clean bathroom equals happy customers.

TO THE SOCIAL MEDIA INTERN who is left with posting boring content like policy changes and adjusted holiday hours, I would say, "Miscommunicating some of the basics to our customers breeds mistrust. If customers don't trust us, they won't buy from us. Your post is important!"

O = OBJECTIVITY

Because this objectivity is so connected to a person's emotional and mental maturity, it is more difficult to provide them with this important strength. How many times have you seen your employees get wound up and spun out by a customer because they were unable to step back and be objective? Find ways to model and reward objectivity.

SOME TIPS:

1. Role-play with employees by creating scenarios that require them to keep their emotions in check (e.g., model a rude customer verbally attacking your employee). Help them navigate these obstacles in training so they can handle the real thing when it comes. And it will come!

2. Help employees think critically! This is becoming a lost art. So many businesses over-systematize their employee tasks to the point that they create inept minions who can't solve problems. Challenge employees to solve daily problems so they can begin to see their role as problem solvers and not just button pushers.

3. Objectivity often comes with perspective, and perspective often comes with time. Give your employees time and room to grow in the area of being objective.

L = LIFT UP AND LEAN ON YOUR EMPLOYEES

LIFT UP YOUR EMPLOYEES IN PUBLIC.

When you compliment your staff in public, you are setting a tone of positivity to other co-workers, managers as well as customers.

1. In the presence of a customer, you can say things like: "You're in good hands with _____. He/she will take good care of you."

2. In the presence of other employees, you can encourage by saying: "I appreciate the extra effort!"

3. In the presence of superiors and co-workers, you can say: "I appreciate all that you have been doing lately."

LEAN ON YOUR EMPLOYEES IN PRIVATE.

One of the biggest mistakes managers make is to criticize an employee in public. This is meant for private conversation away from customer and co-worker eyes and ears. When you take an employee aside, it also communicates that you have something important to discuss. Try some of the examples below when you need to lean on an employee to improve their service:

1. "Let's discuss how you could have handled that situation a little better."

2. "The customer could tell you were irritated. You need to consider how your words and body language communicate what you're really thinking."

3. "I didn't want to say anything negative about you in front of the other employees or customers, but you need to do 'x' differently in the future."

S = SUPPORT THEIR DECISIONS

If you are going to empower your employees, as previously mentioned, it also means that you need to support their decisions. If an employee made a poor decision in an effort to make a customer's day, you need to consider how you can support their intention and train their faulty execution. If you simply reprimand them, they will not take a chance on finding a way to make the customer's day next time. They will begin to play it safe. Celebrate the intention when it's good, and deal separately with the failure in the execution.

Don't put all the responsibility on the manager. Are your frontline employees' hands tied in such a way that they need to contact a manager for every possible concern? If you are relying too much on your manager, customers will soon try to bypass your frontline workers and ask immediately to speak with a manager. This will overload an already-swamped manager and short-circuit any attempts from your hourly employee to be helpful.

YOU NEED TO HIRE WELL.

Let's face it, it is much easier to start with hiring employees that have some of the service qualities we have been discussing. We could spend the rest of the book discussing creative ways to determine your potential employee's service skills.

GO TO: SIXSIDEDSERVICE.COM/FREE
FOR A COPY OF "THE 6 KEYS TO HIRING SERVICE MINDED EMPLOYEES"
TO HELP YOU ASSESS AND HIRE MORE CUSTOMER-CENTRIC EMPLOYEES,

Since the goal is to achieve Customer Relationship Imprinting, the third I.S.S. Trigger—*to develop customer-centric employees by delivering T.O.O.L.S. on a consistent basis*—is pivotal.

If you can flip the switch, the next I.S.S. Trigger may have the greatest influence on your customer impact.

INTERNAL SERVICE SWITCH TRIGGER #4:
DEVELOP CUSTOMER-CENTRIC EMPLOYEES BY HELPING THEM PERSONALIZE CUSTOMER EXPERIENCE

Being customer-centric requires your staff to personalize your customer's experiences.

Treating a customer like a complaint ticket number is a sure way to depersonalize the experience and miss the opportunities for connection.

As you seek to find ways to personalize your customer's experience, it is a good time to remind you of how simple and yet appreciated personalizing your service can be!

I RECENTLY RAN ACROSS A GREAT EXAMPLE OF PERSONALIZING CUSTOMER SERVICE THAT NOT ONLY CREATED MORE RELATIONAL VELCRO BUT WAS PICKED UP AS A NATIONAL STORY THAT WENT VIRAL!

MAY THE FORCE BE WITH YOU.

John, a Star Wars fan and LEGO® builder, recently purchased an impossible-to-find, $350, 3,000-piece Star Wars LEGO® set. After looking at the 400-page instruction booklet, John discovered an entire bag of pieces was missing from this brand-new, hard-to-find set. He contacted LEGO® through the customer service portal on their website.

RATHER THAN RECEIVING A TICKET NUMBER, CANNED RESPONSE OR CHATBOT SEQUENCE, JOHN RECEIVED THIS PERSONALIZED RESPONSE:

"Dear John,

Thanks for getting in touch with us and providing that information! I am so sorry that you are missing bag 14 from your Mos Eisley Cantina! This must be the work of Lord Vader.

Fear not, for I have hired Han to get that bag right out to you. Your order will be arriving in the next 7–10 days (or less the [sic] 12 parsecs). Have a bricktastic day and may the force be with you."[13]

KUDOS TO THIS LEGO® EMPLOYEE.

This employee did more than acknowledge the issue, solve the problem and give a timeframe for the replacement parts. This customer service worker, obviously a Star Wars fan too, used their insight to provide some levity, shared the solution in Star Wars-oriented language to personalize the experience, and built some Relational Velcro along the way.

THAT'S NICE, BUT IS PERSONALIZATION REALLY THAT IMPORTANT?

YES!

THINK ABOUT THIS:

"Thirty-three percent of customers who abandoned a business relationship last year did so because personalization was lacking."[14]

Wow!

ONE-THIRD OF THE CUSTOMERS WHO LEFT YOUR BUSINESS DID SO BECAUSE YOU WEREN'T PERSONAL ENOUGH!

But this also means that you could gain 33% of your competitors' customers who left due to the lack of their personalization.

WHICH SIDE OF THIS EQUATION WILL YOU BE ON?

REPEAT THIS PHRASE:

"THE MORE DIGITAL WE GET, THE MORE PERSONAL WE MUST BECOME!"

If your business is 100% online, you are especially in danger of getting less personal and of your customers "swiping left" and looking for a competitor that relates to them more personally.

A good question for your frontline employees and leadership is:

"WHAT DID WE DO YESTERDAY THAT WILL PERSONALIZE THE SHOPPING EXPERIENCE OF OUR CUSTOMERS TODAY?"

It's also something you may want to ask your customers! The more digital we get, the more personal we must become. Those who personalize and humanize the digital experience win!

WHEN YOU GET PERSONAL, YOU REAP THE REWARDS.

- **AWAY LUGGAGE** | Customers drive every decision made by the company, and Away uses data to create comprehensive customer profiles for personalized recommendations and service.

- **TRIBUTE HOTELS** | Each exclusive hotel in the network has a unique feel for a one-of-a-kind experience that extends beyond just the room to service that meets guests' every need.

- **SEPHORA** | The beauty brand uses technology to create a personalized experience with a comprehensive app, virtual try-on of makeup products and a strong online community for a seamless customer experience.

- **PORSCHE** | The luxury car manufacturer tops the list of customer satisfaction because of its personalized sales approach and quality products.[15]

If you are going to achieve Customer Relationship Imprinting, it means that you need to develop customer-centric employees through personalization, but also through helping them care.

SOMETIMES CARING NEEDS COAXING!

INTERNAL SERVICE SWITCH TRIGGER #5
DEVELOP CUSTOMER-CENTRIC EMPLOYEES BY SHOWING THEM HOW TO C.A.R.E.

This means that it will be most effectively embraced by your staff if they see you modeling C.A.R.E. and not just teaching it. Your staff will know if you really care or if you are just trying to get them to do what you want.

When I wore a younger man's shoes, I was a youth pastor.

You learn quickly working with teens that kids can smell inauthenticity a mile away. We used to have a saying among pastors,

"YOU CAN CON A CON, YOU CAN FOOL A FOOL, BUT YOU CAN'T KID A KID!"

33% OF CUSTOMERS WHO ABANDONED A BUSINESS RELATIONSHIP LAST YEAR DID SO BECAUSE PERSONALIZATION WAS LACKING.

" THE MORE DIGITAL WE GET, THE MORE PERSONAL WE MUST BECOME. "

Michael Barnett

CUSTOMER RELATIONSHIP IMPRINTING

Your staff also know when you're asking them to care in ways that you don't. If they don't think you care, they will sniff it out quickly, and you will not get their complete trust or effort.

Why is all this so important?

BECAUSE CARING PUTS OUR SERVICE IN AN ENTIRELY DIFFERENT CATEGORY.

Customer-centric employees that have the I.S.S. turned on have also engaged empathy, expectation, and critical thinking to provide superior service. So how do you help your people catch a case of caring? Here's a quick way to engage the service switch and help prompt your employees to exercise the behavior of caring that will hopefully become an instinct.

MODEL, MEMORIZE, AND IMPLEMENT.

Have your Service Architects model C.A.R.E., require your team to memorize the C.A.R.E. acrostic, and then help your frontline employees implement C.A.R.E.

C = CONSIDER THE CUSTOMER'S DESIRE, DILEMMA OR DISAPPOINTMENT
Is there a question to answer, a problem to solve or an issue to resolve?

A = AIM TO MAKE THEIR DAY
What can be done to exceed the customer's expectations?

R = READ THE CUSTOMER'S CUES AND BODY LANGUAGE
Is this customer in a hurry...happy...upset...excited...annoyed?

E = ELEVATE THE CUSTOMER'S EXPECTATIONS
What can be done to build trust and confidence with this customer?

I'VE CREATED A FREE "SERVICE C.A.R.E. SHEET" FOR YOU.

The Service C.A.R.E. Sheet is a free resource for your employees to specifically cite examples of how they provided C.A.R.E. to your customers.

 GO TO: SIXSIDEDSERVICE.COM/FREE
FOR A FREE COPY OF "THE SERVICE C.A.R.E. SHEET."

You should make a habit of giving the C.A.R.E. Sheet as a last task in your employee's workday. Periodically, you should review their completed C.A.R.E. Sheets and provide the appropriate affirmation, commentary and training. We need to measure what matters!

CONGRATULATIONS!
YOU MADE IT TO THE END OF THE LONGEST CHAPTER IN THIS BOOK!

This is the longest chapter for a reason. Developing customer-centric employees is no small task. Engaging your employees' Internal Service Switch involves a lot. I hope you will take advantage of the multiple free resources in this chapter.

Remember, you can best develop customer-centric employees when you flip the Internal Service Switch and turn on customer-centric thinking by:

- Using the Reticular Activating System to your advantage.
- Delivering value-based communication.
- Creating service rituals.
- Providing your employees with the T.O.O.L.S. they need.
- Personalizing your customer's service experiences.

- Modeling and showing employees how to C.A.R.E.

Remember the goal!

It's important that you remain focused on the objective of every section in this book, which is to achieve Customer Relationship Imprinting with each and every person who chooses your business to interact with.

Do you remember the definition of Customer Relationship Imprinting?

CUSTOMER RELATIONSHIP IMPRINTING IS "THE ABILITY TO ATTRACT, ACQUIRE, AND RETAIN MORE CUSTOMERS WHO FOLLOW YOU REGARDLESS OF CIRCUMSTANCES."

You must provide power to your employees' Internal Service Switches through the principles covered in this section. This side of your Six-Sided Service is the most demanding and requires the most attention out of all 6 of the CRI elements. But developing customer-centric employees is also the most rewarding element of them all! As you help employees to be more engaging, you will increase the attraction, acquisition and retention of customers. It's worth the effort!

WITH THAT SAID...

THE NEXT ELEMENT IS DIFFERENT THAN ALL THE REST. LIKE A MATCH AND A FUSE, THE COMBINATION WILL EITHER IGNITE YOUR SERVICE OR BURN IT DOWN!

SECTION THREE:
PRACTICAL APPLICATION

DEVELOP CUSTOMER-CENTRIC EMPLOYEES

CRI LEXICON
Key words or phrases from this section

"DEVELOP CUSTOMER-CENTRIC EMPLOYEES" - THE INTERNAL SERVICE SWITCH -
THE RETICULAR ACTIVATING SYSTEM - I.S.S. TRIGGERS ARE VALUE-BASED PROMPTS OR CUES -
"THE MORE DIGITAL WE GET, THE MORE PERSONAL WE MUST BECOME!"

PRACTICAL IMPRESSIONS
Practical questions & exercises from this section for personal application

#1   SURVEY YOUR EMPLOYEES IN THE NEXT TWO WEEKS AND ASK, "WHAT
SHOULD OUR COMPANY VALUE MORE/LESS AND HOW DO YOU RECOMMEND
THAT WE DO THIS?" USE THE DATA TO CREATE TRIGGERS & RITUALS.

Go to: SixSidedService.com for 9 more questions/exercises from section three.

GROUP THERAPY SESSION
For group reading, team building and group discussion

#1   AS A GROUP, GO THROUGH THE T.O.O.L.S. PORTION OF THIS SECTION.
ASSIGN MEMBERS OF THE GROUP TO DEVELOP AN IMPLEMENTATION
STRATEGY FOR EACH AREA OF THE T.O.O.L.S. ACROSTIC.

Go to: SixSidedService.com for 9 more group questions/exercises from section three.

IMPRINT ACCESS
Get more imprinting tools & exclusive content

Text me directly at: **949.577.8397** and I will not only respond to you, but you'll
become a part of my exclusive Imprint Access community. Being part of this group
gives you access to free CRI content, exclusive offers, discounts and more!

CUSTOMER RELATIONSHIP IMPRINTING

The ability to attract, acquire and retain more customers who follow you regardless of circumstances

1. FIND A WAY TO MAKE YOUR CUSTOMER'S DAY

2. ENLIST & EMPOWER SERVICE ARCHITECTS

3. DEVELOP CUSTOMER-CENTRIC EMPLOYEES

4. TREAT BRAND & SERVICE AS INSEPARABLE

5.

6.

MATCH

THE COMBINATION THAT WILL

& FUSE

IGNITE YOUR SERVICE OR BURN IT DOWN

CUSTOMER RELATIONSHIP IMPRINTING
ELEMENT NUMBER FOUR

MATCH & FUSE

THE COMBINATION THAT WILL IGNITE YOUR SERVICE OR BURN IT DOWN

 CUSTOMER RELATIONSHIP IMPRINTING ELEMENT #4: TREAT BRAND & SERVICE AS INSEPARABLE

ENSURING EXCEPTIONAL SERVICE WITHOUT EXCEPTION MEANS COMBINING YOUR MATCH AND FUSE.

When a fuse at the end of a stick of dynamite and a lit match meet each other, there are explosive consequences (pun intended). Keep these two things separate and you have only the possibility of an explosion.

In this section, you will see that combining brand and service can either ignite your service or burn it down. Your brand and your service working together are combustible. The way you handle this CRI element in your day-to-day business determines if the explosion is profitable or catastrophic.

THE STRENGTH OF WARP & WEFT

Look at the shirt or blouse you're wearing right now (assuming you are not reading this naked, although no judgment here). Look at the fibers of the cloth. If you are looking at a linen top, it is more distinguishable than a cotton shirt, but they both are made the same way.

There are two directions of thread that intersect to create the fabric. These two threads are commonly known in the textile industry as the warp (the vertical threads) and weft (the horizontal threads) that are woven between the vertical lines to create the very fabric of what you are wearing.

You can't have just one direction of thread without having huge holes in your fabric. It's the intertwining of two different threads that creates the strength and integrity of the fabric.

MANY CURRENT CUSTOMER SERVICE MODELS SEE THEIR BRAND (THE WARP) AND THEIR CUSTOMER SERVICE (THE WEFT) AS TWO SEPARATE SPOOLS OF THREAD.

While their paths might cross occasionally with a positive social media campaign that uses customer satisfaction testimonials, they are often not treated as the intertwined fabric that creates a strong and vibrant brand.

HOW OFTEN DO YOUR MARKETING DIRECTOR AND CUSTOMER EXPERIENCE OFFICER MEET TO WORK COLLABORATIVELY?

Do they meet every week...once a month...once a quarter? In many instances, these two entities swim in completely different oceans. In companies that are practicing Customer Relationship Imprinting, they are in the same boat.

Until now, you may not have given a lot of thought to the relationship between your brand and your customer service in this way.

Most brand builders, ad agencies and marketing campaigns do not align themselves with customer service-focused approaches like those suggested here. But those that embrace combining their warp and weft—their brand and their service—will be one step closer to achieving Customer Relationship Imprinting. It is a vital side to our Six-Sided Service cube.

CUSTOMER RELATIONSHIP IMPRINTING ELEMENT #4:

 TREAT BRAND & SERVICE AS INSEPARABLE!

Businesses that experience Customer Relationship Imprinting know that their brand and their service are inseparable, and they use this to their advantage.

If you are going to develop customer relationships beyond transactions, as we previously discussed, you need to understand the marriage of brand and service!

Remember, the goal is Customer *Relationship* Imprinting. Your connection to your customer is a relationship.

There are no divorce options or prenuptial agreements on this one. Your brand and your service are linked together like a marriage, for better or for worse.

IT'S IMPORTANT FIRST TO UNDERSTAND THAT YOUR CUSTOMERS ARE CURRENTLY ALREADY PRACTICING THIS CRI ELEMENT!

The public already is currently treating your brand and your service as inseparable. Smart businesses just realize the power of this...and use it to their advantage.

However, many companies fail to detonate their brand and service to their benefit.

CRI element #1, "Make Your Customer's Day," was an easy idea to connect with. In other sections, we will deal with service culture, service with systems and motivating your staff for service.

These are familiar concepts that are easy to wrap our minds around. The CRI element addressed in this chapter takes a little more effort to unearth. But,

LIKE A DIAMOND DEEP IN THE GROUND, IT IS WORTH ALL THE WORK TO GET IT INTO OUR HANDS.

As you get your hands dirty digging through your service soil for this CRI diamond, you need to realize that you have only two real choices of dealing with the reality that your brand and service are inseparable.

TWO CHOICES

CHOICE #1 is to ignore this fact and run the risk of your brand and service contradicting each other and customers building a narrative that is damaging and deadly to your reputation!

CHOICE #2 is to fervently address any contradictions in your brand promise and service delivery. Developing your service and repositioning your brand promises can help you build a reputation that is customer-centric to its core! When brand and service are seen as inseparable, the mission of your company can become more visible. When brand promises align with service directives, your business can harness the full strength of warp and weft.

THE REAL OWNERS OF YOUR BRAND

To be clear, when we are talking about building a brand, we are not speaking of creating a logo or slogan and finding fonts. These are an invitation into the brand, but a brand is something entirely different.

The term comes from cattle ranchers that "branded" their livestock with their mark to show ownership against thieves or help wandering cows get returned to their rightful owner. We've come to believe that our brand is something along these lines. However, in the 21st century, the meaning of branding has changed substantially.

Consider understanding your company brand, not as your logo, mission, or product, but as the very thing consumers think about your business!

Unlike our rancher predecessors, who used their red-hot steel brand to show ownership, today your brand is the one major company asset companies do NOT own!

Coca-Cola, Nike, McDonald's; brand giants and the smallest of companies; and the company you are employed by do not own their brand.

You can trademark, copyright, and create all the brand guides you want. You don't own it. David Flanagan, in his book *Rudder*, says,

"AT THE END OF THE DAY, NO INDIVIDUAL OR COMPANY ACTUALLY OWNS THEIR BRAND. EVERYONE ELSE DOES."[16]

The public always determines what your brand is and what it's not.

SIMPLY PUT: THE PUBLIC OWNS YOUR BRAND!

In fact, you could say that your brand is best explained as this:

YOUR BRAND IS WHAT EVERYONE ELSE THINKS ABOUT YOUR BUSINESS.

Brand promises are important, as you will see, but your service is the keeper of the promises.

When you think about your brand promises, you should think about this:

YOUR BRAND PROMISES ARE BEING DELIVERED OR DESTROYED EVERY DAY BY YOUR CUSTOMER SERVICE.

Perhaps now you can see how the brand is so closely associated with your customer and why you must treat brand and service as inseparable! Your brand is the result of your customer service...good... bad...acceptable...or exceptional.

Your ability to deliver world-class service tells your customers you keep your (brand) promises. Delivered promises are the foundation for trust.

And trust is at the core of attracting, acquiring and retaining those customers you are trying to serve.

ARE YOU BEGINNING TO SEE HOW YOUR BRAND, OWNED BY YOUR CUSTOMER, AND YOUR SERVICE, DELIVERED TO YOUR CUSTOMER, ARE INSEPARABLE?

WHAT HAPPENS WHEN YOUR CUSTOMERS FEEL REPRESENTED BY YOUR BRAND?

Nike is a great example of a brand that has identified their place in the world and uses their brand position to connect with their customers on a different level than any of their competitors.

No one else in their space comes close to touching them. Their brand is more about moving minds than units of shoes. Although, they do sell a ton of their products. Interestingly, their "brand promise" does not even mention the products they sell, or even the product benefits.

It's because their product is something less tangible.

NIKE PROMISES SOMETHING RELATIONAL.

"Nike exists to bring inspiration and innovation to every athlete in the world."[17]

" YOUR BRAND PROMISES ARE BEING DELIVERED OR DESTROYED EVERY DAY BY YOUR CUSTOMER SERVICE. "

Michael Barnett

CUSTOMER RELATIONSHIP IMPRINTING

They are about elevating their purpose to connect with people on a non-sales level. Nike caused a lot of controversy when they partnered with Colin Kaepernick to promote their mission of social justice. Regardless of how you feel about Nike's position, you certainly know about this partnership.

An important sidenote: since Colin Kaepernick became the face of Nike, their sales increases are in the billions![18]

You may disagree with Nike's strategy, but they are clear—and more importantly, their customers are clear—on what they stand for.

When you think about Nike, it's almost impossible to separate their brand from the topic of social injustice.

During all the Kaepernick frenzy, if you asked a friend, spouse, neighbor or even your grandmother,

"WHAT DO YOU THINK OF NIKE?"
THEIR ANSWER HAD NOTHING TO DO WITH SNEAKERS!

Nike has engaged the world in a dialogue that puts them in an entirely different category than their competitors.

If you were to ask these same people what they think about Adidas, you will hear about shoes!

While the example of Nike could just be seen as combining brand and social causes, Nike communicated something deeper.

THEIR BRAND POSITION WAS MARRIED TO THEIR SERVICE POSITION BY ALIGNING THEIR BRAND TO THOSE WHOM THEY WERE SELECTING TO SERVE.

This is an important distinction. People who felt marginalized raised the Nike banner and aligned themselves with a company that was providing customer service in the form of representation. The way you treat customers, represent their desires (not exclusive to social issues) and identify their service needs fuels the fires of this CRI element.

The way Nike treated their brand and service as inseparable is subtle but effective.
This is the match and fuse, the warp and weft; the eruptive power of treating your brand and your service as inseparable!

Usually, the application questions are left to the end of the section, but I want you to take a minute and consider the following important questions about your business before we continue.

STOP AND ANSWER THESE QUESTIONS:

1. How is your brand different from your competitors'?

2. How are you serving your customers through representation?

3. When people speak about your business, what do they associate your brand with?

Before you read further, write down at least one answer to each of the three questions above.

_____

_____

_____

_____

_____

_____

_____

If your customers describe your brand exclusively in terms of the product or service you sell, then you are missing out on the power that comes with combining your brand and service.

When companies understand, align, and execute customer service directives through their brand, advertising and marketing initiatives, something very special happens.

On the other hand, if you fail to marry your brand and service together positively, you will be like...well...like most everybody else.

This is a problem!

You see, when you are so like your competitors, it's as though you're shooting with identical pistols!

CHOOSE IDENTICAL PISTOLS OR CHOOSE TO WIN.

Once upon a disagreement, victory or defeat was determined by how quickly and accurately you could discharge a bullet at your foe.

IN THE PAST, DUELING WITH PISTOLS WAS A WAY TO RESOLVE SIGNIFICANT DISAGREEMENTS.

Prior to being our president, Andrew Jackson killed a man in a duel for cheating on a bet and insulting his wife![19]

Think about that the next time you pull out a $20 bill with his face on it.

Identical guns leveled the playing field, and your ability, or lack thereof, was the main difference between life and death.

TODAY WE LIVE IN A WORLD OF KEYBOARD COURAGE.

Everyone gets really brave typing insults, accusations or challenges from behind their computer screen.

WHAT IF TODAY YOU HAD TO BACK UP YOUR SOCIAL MEDIA COMMENTS BY MEETING THE RECIPIENT OF YOUR BRAVADO WITH PISTOLS AT DAWN?

There may be a bit more respect if this was the case. Feel free to add this suggestion to your next social media post.

Your current organization is likely selling the same product or service as most of your competitors.

Of course, your service or product is better than the competition's, but come along with me for a moment in assuming the services and products you provide are, at the very least, similar to your competitors'.

YOU AND YOUR COMPETITORS HAVE IDENTICAL PISTOLS.

While price, convenience, availability and quality are still key ingredients to being competitive in today's marketplace, it's the superior exceptional customer service that differentiates your business from your competition when other facets are similar.

Don't forget about the previously covered 17% Factor!

If you have exceptional customer service and can leverage your brand to communicate the service differences to your customer, your competitors will lose.

WHEN YOU ENGAGE THE WARP AND THE WEFT, YOU ARE ARMING YOURSELF WITH SOMETHING UNIQUELY DIFFERENT THAN YOUR COMPETITION.

YOU NOW ARE SHOOTING WITH AN ENTIRELY DIFFERENT WEAPON.

You're no longer shooting with identical pistols...and the result is that you win every time!

When you treat your brand and service as inseparable, you are armed with greater and more effective artillery than your competitors, or...would you rather have a fair fight?

You choose...identical pistols or winning!

YOUR SERVICE REFLECTS AND REPRESENTS YOUR BRAND. IF YOU HAVE A GREAT BRAND BUT LOUSY SERVICE, THEN YOU HAVE A LOUSY BRAND. PERIOD!

FOR A MINUTE, IMAGINE THAT YOU WORK FOR TESLA.

You're ready to launch an unbelievable new line of products. Millions of dollars and thousands of labor hours have been put into this project. As part of Tesla, you are delivering a new technology that is light-years ahead of your competitors' technology.

The quality and price of the product is on point. After releasing this great product, you would likely hear from the masses and the media about how great and innovative the Tesla brand is.

Another victory, right?

However, if your customers can't get a Tesla customer service representative to pick up the phone, a chatbot response or an email answered about a product or billing issue, the media and the masses would describe the Tesla brand differently.

If Elon Musk's service center "ghosted" customers and didn't respond to them or took way too long to resolve issues, the public opinion of your *brand* would change.

INNOVATION DOESN'T MATTER WHEN THE BRAND BEHIND IT DOESN'T SUPPORT ITS CUSTOMERS.

If enough people have a bad customer service experience, they will relate it to a poor *brand* experience.

WHY?

BECAUSE YOUR BRAND AND YOUR SERVICE ARE INSEPARABLE.

This is the combustible result of match and fuse and "treating brand and service as inseparable."

THIS IS WHAT BEGINS TO SEPARATE THOSE SERIOUS ABOUT BUILDING CUSTOMER RELATIONSHIPS FROM ORGANIZATIONS THAT DABBLE IN IMPROVING THEIR CUSTOMER SERVICE EXPERIENCES.

Your ability to develop Customer Relationship Imprinting is determined, in part, by your mastery of treating brand and service as inseparable.

UNTAPPED OPPORTUNITIES

When you realize the public owns your brand, you can find some untapped opportunities if you just listen to what these brand owners are saying about you.

Asking the right questions is the key to building a brand. The right questions have helped companies find their brand differentiators from their competitors, avoid overpromising, chart a new business course, or uncover who they are trying to be in the world.

One of the exercises that these companies do is have every single employee—from the president to the janitor—fill out a questionnaire before they begin building and defining a brand. They include questions like "What is the greatest strength of your company?" and "What do customers say regularly about your business?"

How would *your* senior staff, frontline employees and customers answer these questions?

In one session with a client, I had an experience that I had not had before and have not had since.

WITHOUT EXCEPTION, EVERY EMPLOYEE IN THE GROUP I WAS WORKING WITH, INCLUDING THE JANITOR, SAID, "OUR CUSTOMERS AND EMPLOYEES ARE ALL LIKE FAMILY."

Consumers who shopped this brand were then polled, and they overwhelmingly gravitated toward appreciating the family feel they experienced as a customer. Some even added a note mentioning that they felt more like family than a customer.

AND THIS IS A NATIONAL BRAND!

The example of Nike revealed how your brand selects *whom* you serve, but this experience highlights *how* those receiving your service feel about the service you're delivering.

This is another critical piece of treating brand and service as inseparable.

OH MY...IT WORKS!

The interesting thing was that before this discovery, the senior management of this corporation believed they should market their products from a lower price position. They were mistakenly believing that their customers would buy more if they positioned themselves as the low-price leader. Their brand is a nationally recognized household brand, but they missed the true source of connectivity.

THEY WERE MISSING THE WARP AND THE WEFT CONNECTION AND THEREFORE MISSING THE OPPORTUNITY TO IGNITE THEIR SERVICE.

The real strength of this brand was the customer relationships that their staff had developed and nurtured. It was time to align the warp and the weft. We focused all the TV spots, social media campaigns and retail promotions around a "you are family" approach.

THEY WERE SITTING ON THE WINNING LOTTERY TICKET AND DIDN'T EVEN KNOW IT!

What happened next?

WITHIN 11 MONTHS, THERE WERE DOUBLE-DIGIT INCREASES IN GROSS SALES!

They didn't lower a single price. Instead, they took what customers already believed about their brand (warp) and simply aligned the brand belief with the customer service (weft) strength.

Why did they see such large increases?

They harnessed the power that comes through using the warp (brand) and the weft (service) together. Some would just say that this is just good brand positioning, but it's really learning to "Treat Brand & Service as Inseparable."

BURNING DOWN YOUR SERVICE:
WHEN THE COMBINATION OF YOUR BRAND AND SERVICE HAS DISASTROUS RESULTS.

In the beginning of this section, I noted that the match and fuse of combining your brand and service can also have disastrous results.

We've discussed the positive impact that the combination of your brand and service have when seen as inseparable, but there is a flipside to this. What happens when your brand promises get contradicted by your service?

"FLY THE FRIENDLY SKIES"
WAS UNITED AIRLINES' PROMISE TO CUSTOMERS.

It was a popular, memorable and regularly stated brand promise of this airline giant that served them well. But something occurred at United that reminded everyone how disastrous being on the wrong side of this Customer Relationship Imprinting element can be!

"United Airlines suffered the pinnacle of all social media crises when a video of law enforcement officers dragging a passenger forcibly off one of its planes went viral and was viewed online more than 200 million times.

Three weeks after United Airlines' spectacular customer experience disaster, customers received a letter from the company's CEO, Oscar Munoz, that began with acknowledging the brand's broken promise to customers:

'Each flight you take with us represents an important promise we make to you, our customer,' the letter read. 'It's not simply that we make sure you reach your destination safely and on time, but also that you will be treated with the highest level of service and the deepest sense of dignity and respect.'

United failed to uphold its brand promise on multiple levels: From the fundamental promise of delivering the service paid for, to providing customer safety, to treating passengers respectfully and delivering on the aspirational promise found in its 'Fly the friendly skies' tagline."[20]

TO BE FAIR, THERE IS NO SUCH THING AS PERFECT SERVICE.
BAD SERVICE HAPPENS.

In a world where every customer is armed with a video camera and the ability to instantly share, hashtag and tag, you will want to make sure your service is not contradicting your brand promises.

THIS IS WHY TRAINING IS SO VITAL TO YOUR SERVICE MISSION.

I imagine United Airlines looked a lot closer at their customer service training, service deficiencies and warning signs after this incident.

REMEMBER: THE COMBINATION OF YOUR BRAND AND SERVICE WILL IGNITE YOUR SERVICE OR BURN IT DOWN!

Don't wait until you must release a statement on your service failures to make service changes.

MANY "BRAND PROMISES" HAVE BEEN BROKEN BY PUBLIC OPINION!

Your brand promises will build or erode your customer's trust in you. What if you keep breaking your brand promises?

A Gallup poll taken several years ago discovered "less than half of current customers felt that the brands they use keep the promises they make."[21]

Just keeping your brand promises will keep you ahead of your competitors and build trust with your customers. This helps you not only retain customers but attract new ones—because customer acquisition follows a good reputation.

Take a minute and write here what a few of your company's brand promises are:

_____

_____

_____

_____

_____

_____

IT IS CRITICAL THAT YOUR ACTIONS DON'T CONTRADICT YOUR PROMISES.

Your spouse or kids may forgive you, but the owners of your brand (your customers) may have a more difficult time and it may cost you dearly.

Is this an overstatement? No! This is worth repeating:

YOUR BRAND PROMISES ARE DELIVERED OR DESTROYED EVERY DAY BY YOUR CUSTOMER SERVICE.

It is crucial that you are not confused about the role your customer service and customer experience play in your brand.

The sum total of your customer experiences equals your true brand position!

What are you promising customers, or what do customers expect from you?

CAN YOUR SERVICE HOLD THE WEIGHT OF YOUR BRAND PROMISES?

As I mentioned in the beginning of this section, this element is different than the other five. It is that diamond worth digging up, but don't be fooled—the more you polish this CRI element, the more your brand and service will serve you as you serve your customers.

FOR THE FIRST FOUR ELEMENTS, WE'VE BEEN LOOKING AT ATTRACTING, ACQUIRING AND RETAINING YOUR CUSTOMERS, BUT THE NEXT SECTION IS ABOUT DEVELOPING THE DNA OF YOUR INTERNAL CULTURE.

If you are feeding a service culture that embraces your staff, then you are creating an inviting environment for new hires and making it difficult for long-time employees to leave.

Simply put: what you feed is what will lead!

IN ORDER TO CREATE THIS TYPE OF CULTURE, YOU WILL NEED TO UNDERSTAND HOW TO NURTURE THE CULTURE.

SECTION FOUR:
PRACTICAL APPLICATION

TREAT BRAND
& SERVICE AS
INSEPARABLE

CRI LEXICON
Key words or phrases from this section

"TREAT BRAND & SERVICE AS INSEPARABLE" - WARP & WEFT - "THE PUBLIC OWNS YOUR BRAND" - "YOUR BRAND PROMISES ARE BEING DELIVERED OR DESTROYED EVERY DAY BY YOUR CUSTOMER SERVICE" - "CHOOSE IDENTICAL PISTOLS OR CHOOSE TO WIN"

PRACTICAL IMPRESSIONS
Practical questions & exercises from this section for personal application

#1 WHAT ARE 5 WAYS YOUR BRAND PROMISES ARE BEING DELIVERED BY YOUR SERVICE? WHAT ARE 3 WAYS YOUR BRAND PROMISES ARE BEING DESTROYED BY YOUR SERVICE?

Go to: SixSidedService.com for 9 more questions/exercises from section four.

GROUP THERAPY SESSION
For group reading, team building and group discussion

#1 HAVE EVERYONE IN YOUR GROUP NAME 3 HOUSEHOLD BRANDS & COLLECTIVELY CREATE A LIST OF THE WARP & WEFT OF EACH BRAND. NEXT, HAVE EVERYONE DO THE SAME WITH YOUR BRAND. THEN DISCUSS!

Go to: SixSidedService.com for 9 more group questions/exercises from section four.

IMPRINT ACCESS
Get more imprinting tools & exclusive content

Text me directly at: **949.577.8397** and I will not only respond to you, but you'll become a part of my exclusive Imprint Access community. Being part of this group gives you access to free CRI content, exclusive offers, discounts and more!

FIND A WAY TO MAKE YOUR CUSTOMER'S DAY

1

ENLIST & EMPOWER SERVICE ARCHITECTS

2

DEVELOP CUSTOMER-CENTRIC EMPLOYEES

3

TREAT BRAND & SERVICE AS INSEPARABLE

4

NURTURE THE CULTURE

5

6

CUSTOMER RELATIONSHIP IMPRINTING

The ability to attract, acquire and retain more customers who follow you regardless of circumstances

5

WHAT YOU FEED

THE HIDDEN FACTORS THAT FEED

IS WHAT WILL LEAD

OR STARVE YOUR SERVICE DNA

CUSTOMER RELATIONSHIP IMPRINTING
ELEMENT NUMBER FIVE

WHAT YOU FEED IS WHAT WILL LEAD

THE HIDDEN FACTORS THAT FEED OR STARVE YOUR SERVICE DNA

 **CUSTOMER RELATIONSHIP IMPRINTING ELEMENT #5: NURTURE THE CULTURE**

YOUR "TRIBE" NEEDS TO READ THIS.

There's an old Native American story that I'd like to introduce you to.

A powerful tribal chief had been concerned about what he had recently noticed with the young children of his tribe. A few of his younger tribal members were headed down the wrong path in life. They were influencing the other children and making poor decisions and treating each other harshly and spreading negativity like a disease. Day after day, the chief saw this behavior and the ongoing decisions to make the wrong choice.

He knew something needed to be done. The chief decided to gather all the tribe's children to address his concerns. The young Native American children were summoned to meet with their leader. Every one of them, with great anticipation, gathered to hear what their chief had to say.

Since it was not a regular occurrence that their chief would want to speak with them directly, they had no idea what to expect him to say or do.

As chief, he could order them to stop treating each other so harshly. But he knew that this would not get to the core of the issue. He would only be altering their behavior and not their character. So, to reach their hearts and minds, he simply needed to share the following illustration with them.

Looking into the eyes of the young faces transfixed on their leader, the chief shared this short but powerful insight:

"There are two dogs in my head. One always wants to do the right thing and the other one always wants to do the wrong thing. The two dogs in my mind are always fighting. They never stop.

But I have learned how to help one dog win the fight and the other dog to lose the fight.

The dog that wins...is the one that I feed the most."

Right now, there is a fight happening inside the walls of your business. Even if the walls are virtual, the fight is real. The dog fight is a battle for your company culture.

On one side is a positive, mission-oriented, people-first focus that creates a thriving service culture. On the other side of the fight is the exact opposite.

The winner of this war belongs to the culture that you feed the most. And the loser will be the culture that you weaken through starvation!

WHICH "DOG" IS YOUR LEADERSHIP AND SUPPORT STAFF FEEDING AND WHICH ARE THEY STARVING?

The human body enables every organ to function at full capacity when all the right nutrients are consumed and distributed.

Your internal culture is the same way. If you are feeding your employees a nutrient-dense diet of support, mission-first initiatives and a people-centric approach, your system will produce healthy results.

The opposite is also true. If you starve your staff and create a nutrient-deficient culture, like any organism, they will only operate in survival mode, conserving all their energy for the basic tasks of their job.

I want to be as clear as I can:

WHAT YOU FEED IS WHAT WILL LEAD!

As with a living, breathing creature, the fuel you feed it determines what you grow! As you feed what you lead, you are growing your internal work culture.

Consequently, the employee culture or community you create internally has an impact on the service you provide externally. If you have a negative work environment, unhappy employees and a lack of mission within your organization, your customers will eventually experience it. If you see a dysfunctional internal mess, where employees are devalued, disengaged and underdeveloped, you will also see an environment in which it is almost impossible to provide consistent world-class service experiences for customers. Your internal culture is also an indicator of your external capabilities.

But before we jump into discovering how to nurture your internal culture, you need to know about the three hidden factors that impact your team.

HIDDEN FACTORS THAT FEED OR STARVE YOUR SERVICE DNA

There are factors hidden in plain sight within your company. They will feed your service DNA or, if ignored, will starve the very organism you are trying to grow.

HIDDEN FACTOR #1
THE LAW OF THE TRIPLE IMPACT IS AT WORK EVERY DAY IN YOUR BUSINESS.

Regardless of what type of business you are in, there are three sectors of impact that can elevate or devastate your business.

I call these three areas of impact "the Law of the Triple Impact"!

THE LAW OF THE TRIPLE IMPACT IS:

All your customer service activity, inactivity, excellence or subpar efforts always exponentially impact three areas of your business:

#1 | Your customers
#2 | Your company
#3 | Your community (social media, online presence, reputation)

You may be thinking, "I know this!" Well, I waited to bring this up in this section because your culture has more sway over the Law of the Triple Impact than any other area of your business.

Remember that culture and community carry the loudest voice to your customers, your company (employees) and the community. Consider using the Law of the Triple Impact as a measuring tool for your culture efforts.

HIDDEN FACTOR #2
YOUR CULTURE IS THE RESULT OF WHO AND WHAT YOU REWARD.

Say this out loud to yourself:

"Our culture is the result of who and what we reward."

THIS REALITY WILL ELICIT CELEBRATION OR CONCERN!

There are personalities that are applauded and others that are ignored. So, the real question is, which traits are rewarded, developed and celebrated at your organization? These are the traits that will take the lead in your culture.

REMEMBER, WHATEVER GETS CELEBRATED, REPEATED AND DEVELOPED IS THE "DOG" YOU ARE FEEDING.

Take a survey among your employees to help you determine the condition of your culture. Ask your staff, "Who and what gets rewarded at our company?"

You may be surprised at the results.

Can you and I agree on something?

HIDDEN FACTOR #3
YOU MUST CREATE A CULTURE, NOT A PROGRAM.

" SAY THIS OUT LOUD TO YOURSELF: 'OUR CULTURE IS THE RESULT OF WHO & WHAT WE REWARD.' "

Michael Barnett

CUSTOMER RELATIONSHIP IMPRINTING

YOU DON'T NEED ANOTHER PROGRAM!

Culture is not fixed by a program or a few team exercises. If you are reading *Customer Relationship Imprinting* in order to just get a few ideas for your service program, you are missing the point. You need to take the time to deepen customer service experiences by strengthening your culture.

TO DEVELOP THE SERVICE CULTURE YOU'RE TRYING TO DELIVER EXTERNALLY, YOU'LL NEED TO NURTURE YOUR INTERNAL EMPLOYEE CULTURE.

BLAH, BLAH, BLAH!

Some say, "There is an overemphasis on corporate culture... what does it have to do with the service abilities that my employees provide?"

THE ANSWER IS, EVERYTHING.

The economist Peter Drucker famously said,

"CULTURE EATS STRATEGY FOR BREAKFAST."

I'll add,

"ONCE YOUR INTERNAL CULTURE IS FINISHED EATING STRATEGY FOR BREAKFAST, AS YOU SWALLOW, THE QUALITY OF WHAT YOU'RE FEEDING YOUR CULTURE WILL EITHER NOURISH OR DEPLETE YOUR ENTIRE SYSTEM, PROVIDING ENERGY OR TOXINS TO EVERYTHING YOU DO."

Not quite as succinct as Mr. Drucker, but worth your consideration.

This brings us to the fifth CRI element commonly held by other businesses that consistently deliver exceptional service without exception.

CUSTOMER RELATIONSHIP IMPRINTING ELEMENT #5
 NURTURE THE CULTURE

CORPORATE CULTURE LESSONS FROM THE THIRD GRADE

Sometimes we need to look backward to move forward. Let's look deeper inside the internal culture you are creating.

Several years ago, my youngest daughter was starting the third grade. Like most young parents, I was interested in meeting and learning about the teacher who would be shaping my daughter's worldview. His name was Mr. K. He ended up being the type of teacher that movies are made of. He celebrated the innocence of third graders, sang songs on his keyboard, and was the Mister Rogers of the school district.

Out of all the things about "Mr. K" that are memorable, there is something he said that is relevant to our conversation about creating and guiding your company's culture.

For full effect, you may want to read the following in a Mister Rogers voice in your head:

"KIDS, I CAN'T CONTROL WHAT HAPPENS OUTSIDE MY CLASS, BUT WE CAN CREATE SOMETHING SPECIAL INSIDE OUR CLASS."

As a Service Architect, you are in a position to do "something special inside your class (business)."

The truth is that you can't change a lot in the culture around you. However, you can change the culture within the organization that you are a part of.

By definition, culture is:

"a way of life of a group of people—the behaviors, beliefs, values, and symbols that they accept, generally without thinking about them, and that are passed along by communication and imitation from one generation to the next. Culture is symbolic communication."[22]

Your customer service needs to flow out of the culture of your in-house relationships, policies and principles.

You were previously introduced to the Internal Service Switch (the ability to turn on customer-centric thinking). The same principles of using value-based communication and creating service rituals apply to nurturing your culture. There is a rhythm and flow to the place you work. There are acceptable norms that may not be acceptable at other businesses. There is a stated and unstated code of conduct.

Values ooze out of the cells of those you work alongside. Think of every intra-office interaction as an opportunity to feed the culture that you are growing.

#1 | NURTURE THE CULTURE BY CREATING A MISSION MINDSET.

IS YOUR MISSION WORTH YOUR TEAM'S TIME, TALENT AND DAILY COMMITMENT?

What happens when you give your staff something more to work for than a check?

The culture you are seeking often takes shape when there is a focus on a greater mission than just the selling of goods and services. You need to be clear, beyond profit and expansion, on what you want your employees to care about and connect with.

YEARS AGO, STEVE JOBS DID WHAT NO ONE ELSE COULD DO.

No, I'm not referring to changing the face of technology. We all know that.

THIS IS A DIFFERENT STORY.

There is a lesser-known story worth sharing with you here. Jobs convinced the president of Pepsi to leave the lucrative global company to join Apple.

He didn't try to lure him with more money, or more exciting products, or even a bigger and better brand.

So, how did Jobs convince John Sculley to walk away from a job that took a lifetime to climb to?

He focused Sculley on the mission of Apple.

Sitting on a balcony overlooking Central Park, Steve Jobs looked at John Sculley and said,

"Do you want to sell sugar water for the rest of your life or come with me and change the world?"

Jobs gave Sculley a mission worth his time, talent, and commitment. What mission are you giving your staff that's worth following?

GREAT SERVICE TENDS TO FLOW MORE NATURALLY WHEN ACCOMPANIED BY A MISSION-BASED CULTURE.

If you are creating a healthy community culture, then you will be fostering an environment where people know they are making a difference in the lives they encounter.

WHAT'S THE GREATER MISSION OF YOUR BUSINESS?

_____

_____

_____

_____

_____

DO ALL YOUR EMPLOYEES KNOW YOUR MISSION?

This is more than "cause marketing." However, companies like TOMS Shoes, which gives away one pair of shoes to Third World recipients for every pair of shoes they sell in the United States, have found that mission and culture go hand in hand.

I have had the privilege of speaking with several men and women who lived through World War II. Some tell stories of selling war bonds, working in factories to build assets for the war, or fighting on the front lines. Regardless of what these heroes did, they all end up saying the same thing in one way or another: "We did whatever we could do to help win the war." They had a clear mission.

THEIR CULTURE WAS TRANSFORMED BECAUSE THE MISSION WAS CLEAR.

Am I being overly dramatic about your culture?

Maybe, but unless you believe in the mission of your business beyond the dollars and help those around you see the mission, you will just be like 85% of your competitors that focus only on providing goods and service faster, cheaper and more conveniently.

Your culture and your service become something entirely different when your team is focused on a mission larger than making a sale. If your team feels connected to your mission, it is much more likely that their excitement for what you've created will rub off on your customers. Like fresh converts, they will want to tell those closest to them, as well as your customers, all that your company is doing collectively to support a greater cause.

You are developing your internal relationships with character, principle, care and consideration. Those who peek inside will see you are building a community.

TODAY, THIS EMPHASIS MATTERS MORE THAN EVER!

A good Service Architect knows that nurturing the culture begins by giving your team a mission worth their time, talent and daily commitment.

#2 | NURTURE THE CULTURE BY TREATING KINDNESS AS CURRENCY.

HOW DO YOU REWARD AND VALUE KINDNESS ON A REGULAR BASIS?

As a young twenty-something, I worked for a company that had sales reps come in on a weekly basis to discuss supply purchases. This was before online ordering was even a blip on your auto-order screen.

The company I worked for was the largest of its kind in the United States. They were a sales rep's dream. A busy business that needed many supplies.

Can you say sales commissions?

Stan, Jim, Edward and Rick were reps from different companies. Each week I would see them walk in wearing suits and looking for the buyer at our company.

They would often be in my work area waiting for their big buyer. I was an hourly employee with no power or importance to these busy salesmen. All these reps had no time even to speak with me.

TO THEM I WAS OF LITTLE VALUE.

All, except Rick. He would always come say "hello" to me before or after he finished his sales call. He was kind. He took the time to ask about my interests, even though I could not benefit him financially or professionally.

Fast-forward a few years.

The day came, surprisingly to me, that I was asked to become the new buyer! I was now in charge of all the purchasing for the business. I remember vividly the week I was promoted. Stan, Jim and Edward would walk in separately to do their usual business with the buyer. They were told by the receptionist that I was their new contact for any supply purchases. Suddenly, these three were glad to see me! I was now of some value to them.

THEY HAD CREATED A CLASS SYSTEM IN THEIR MINDS. I HAD BEEN IN THE LOWER CLASS, AND THEY WERE IN A HIGHER CLASS.

But now, in their estimation, I had graduated to be on their level. It's easy to do this. In the business of getting things done, you can easily overlook those who aren't part of your department, sales or business interactions.

IF YOU WANT TO KNOW HOW YOUR STAFF REALLY TREATS PEOPLE, ASK YOUR COMPANY'S JANITOR OR SECURITY GUARD. THEY KNOW!

In that same week, Rick came looking to speak with the buyer! When he found out that I was the new buyer, he genuinely congratulated me.

BUT WAIT...THERE'S MORE!

My supervisor knew of Rick's attentiveness to all his employees, so he gave me some surprising instructions:

"GIVE RICK ALL OF OUR ORDERS."

"I want to send a message to these other businesses...and to Rick." I told Rick that he was getting all our orders, not just for this week, but for the next several months.

I was asked to tell him the following:

"YOU CARE ABOUT PEOPLE AND OUR COMPANY WANTS TO DO BUSINESS WITH COMPANIES THAT VALUE PEOPLE!"

To say Rick was surprised would be an understatement. He just smiled and said,

"Well Mike, I didn't expect that, but thank you so much! I'll see you next week."

It was also a bit of a shock for Stan, Jim and Edward.

REMEMBER: KINDNESS IS CURRENCY.
YOU CAN CHOOSE TO BE RICH OR BROKE. IT'S UP TO YOU!

More importantly, being kind shouldn't be a tactic to benefit you financially. True kindness is about doing something for those around you, knowing they can't pay you back!

If you can add to people's lives and not take from them, as well as teach others to do the same thing, you will be on the right path to creating a culture of kindness!

Kindness is a direct path to creating a thriving internal culture that overflows to your external service.

TREAT KINDNESS AS CURRENCY AND BE A BIG SPENDER ON YOUR TEAM!

Too many businesses make their staff collateral damage by treating them unkindly. They often have a great external reputation and a horrible internal reputation.

EMPLOYEES MATTER.

CUSTOMERS MATTER

BE KIND.

" REMEMBER:

KINDNESS IS CURRENCY.

YOU CAN CHOOSE TO BE

RICH OR BROKE.

IT'S UP TO YOU! **"**

Michael Barnett

CUSTOMER RELATIONSHIP IMPRINTING

#3 | NURTURE THE CULTURE BY DEVELOPING THE TEAM AROUND YOU.

HOW ARE YOU DEVELOPING YOUR EMPLOYEES TO THEIR FULL POTENTIAL?

Developing the people around you is healthy. And anything that is healthy will grow. It stands to reason that investing in the growth of your employees is a vital piece of creating a culture of development.

DISCOVER AND DEVELOP HIDDEN TALENT IN YOUR STAFF.

It's often easier to train and develop those who understand your current culture than deal with the culture shock of outsiders entering your new world.

A little sidenote: Don't be surprised if your million-dollar ideas are found with your fifteen-dollar-an-hour employees.

HERE'S A LIST OF JOBS THAT SOME FAMOUS PEOPLE ONCE HELD BEFORE BEING DISCOVERED, FINDING THEIR CALLING, OR DEVELOPING IN THEIR AREA OF EVENTUAL EXPERTISE.

A. This holy man could still be a bouncer at a club.

B. This world-renowned fashion designer could still be figure skating.

C. This financial expert could still be bagging groceries.

D. This rock music icon could still be selling ice cream or working in a psychiatric hospital.

E. This military leader could still be selling baby furniture.

F. This R&B singer could still be counting someone else's money.

* **See answers**

What if these men and women never were discovered, found their calling, or developed in their area of expertise?

SEE WHAT THOSE AROUND YOU CAN DO RATHER THAN WHAT THEY ARE CURRENTLY DOING.

In your company, are you looking at what your employees could be doing in the future or do you see them as they currently are?

What if right now, you have a great employee with incredible potential? This person can impact your business, but you aren't seeing their potential.

IN A FEW YEARS, YOU CAN HAVE THREE POSSIBLE STORIES TO TELL ABOUT NURTURING YOUR CULTURE BY DEVELOPING YOUR EMPLOYEES.

POSSIBLE STORY #1
Five years from now, you can tell the story of how you saw something special in this employee. You will be able to celebrate all the amazing ideas and innovations that he/she has brought to your business.

POSSIBLE STORY #2
You can be a footnote on a great businessman's/woman's *Wikipedia* page and tell new hires that this now-strategic business thinker, entrepreneur or business leader once worked at your company.

POSSIBLE STORY #3
You can have this person remain working for you in a capacity where they'd never reach their full potential. This would be the biggest shame of all. Don't miss opportunities to develop the people around you!

WHICH STORY WILL YOU BE TELLING?

Wouldn't you want to be telling story #1? You say, "Well, of course." Then the real question is this: What are you currently doing to discover and develop talent within your organization, and is it working? If the answer is "yes," then you are on the right path here. If the answer is "no," then you need to start slow and begin to mine for these employees.

* Answers:

A. Pope Francis spent his youth working as a bouncer at a Buenos Aires night club.[23]

B. Before she was one of the world's most famous bridal and fashion designers, Vera Wang was a competitive figure skater. (She was even inducted into the U.S. Figure Skating Hall of Fame.)[24]

C. American investor, business tycoon, philanthropist and the chairman and CEO of Berkshire Hathaway, Warren Buffett is considered one of the most successful investors in the world. He has a net worth of $78.9 billion as of August 2020.[25]

D. Before becoming a musical icon, Mick Jagger sold ice cream. He was also a porter for a psychiatric hospital.[26]

E. Before he was a general or a diplomat, Colin Powell worked in a baby furniture store while growing up in the Bronx, even learning some Yiddish from his employers.[27]

F. John Legend was an accountant before recording hits like "All of Me." After graduating from the University of Pennsylvania, he worked at the Boston Consulting Group for three years, but he could never stop thinking about making music.[28]

HOW DOES THIS FIT INTO CUSTOMER RELATIONSHIP IMPRINTING?

At the beginning of this book, you were given the definition of Customer Relationship Imprinting. As a reminder, it is:

"THE ABILITY TO ATTRACT, ACQUIRE AND RETAIN MORE CUSTOMERS WHO FOLLOW YOU REGARDLESS OF CIRCUMSTANCES."

So, what does nurturing your internal culture have to do with this definition?

Before your staff consistently deliver exceptional service, they will need to know the three things we just covered in this section.

In order to feed the culture you want to grow, you must:

1. Create a mission mindset with every employee.

2. Treat kindness as currency...and spend big.

3. Take time to develop those around you.

ULTIMATELY, CRI ELEMENT #5 IS ABOUT INVESTING IN YOUR PEOPLE. THEY WILL, IN TURN, INVEST IN YOUR CUSTOMERS.

Nurturing your culture by being mission-minded, creating a culture of kindness and taking an interest in developing your staff fits perfectly into your service goals—or at least it should!

If you look at most businesses that are delivering the highest level of service, you will find CRI element #5 embedded deep into the culture and fabric of their staff.

A healthy community is infectious.

INVESTING IN YOUR INTERNAL COMMUNITY ALSO HELPS YOU ATTRACT, ACQUIRE AND RETAIN EMPLOYEES AND NOT JUST CUSTOMERS.

THIS IS THE GIFT OF A HEALTHY CULTURE!

ARE YOU READY TO STEER YOUR SERVICE WITH SYSTEMS?

As you turn the page to discover the final Customer Relationship Imprinting element, waiting for you is the greatest challenge found in every single business attempting to deliver superior service. There isn't a single company that doesn't struggle with this.

What is it?

Consistency.

If you want to ensure exceptional service without exception, you will need consistency.

WITHOUT CONSISTENCY, CUSTOMER RELATIONSHIP IMPRINTING IS JUST A NICE TITLE FOR A BOOK AND A PIPEDREAM FOR YOUR SERVICE FUTURE.

In order to have consistency, you need a system to help you stay on track. The last section is the key to ensuring your service success, recovery and forecasting!

CRI LEXICON
Key words or phrases from this section

"NURTURE THE CULTURE" - "WHAT YOU FEED IS WHAT WILL LEAD" - "YOUR CULTURE IS THE RESULT OF WHO AND WHAT YOU REWARD" - "THE LAW OF THE TRIPLE IMPACT" - "KINDNESS IS CURRENCY" - "DEVELOP A MISSION MINDSET" - "DISCOVER & DEVELOP YOUR HIDDEN TALENT"

PRACTICAL IMPRESSIONS
Practical questions & exercises from this section for personal application

#1 WHAT BEHAVIORS SHOULD YOUR BUSINESS RECOGNIZE AND REWARD MORE THAN YOU DO? WHAT IMPROVEMENTS CAN YOU MAKE TO ENSURE EVERY EMPLOYEE UNDERSTANDS AND SEES THEIR ROLE IN THE GREATER MISSION OF YOUR COMPANY?

Go to: SixSidedService.com for 9 more questions/exercises from section five

GROUP THERAPY SESSION
For group reading, team building and group discussion

#1 AS A GROUP HAVE AN HONEST CONVERSATION ABOUT WHO AND WHAT GETS REWARDED AT THE VARIOUS LEVELS OF YOUR ORGANIZATION. CELEBRATE WHEN YOU'RE GETTING IT RIGHT AND DISCUSS HOW TO FIX THE ERRORS.

Go to: SixSidedService.com for 9 more group questions/exercises from section five.

IMPRINT ACCESS

Get more imprinting tools & exclusive content

Text me directly at: **949.577.8397** and I will not only respond to you, but you'll become a part of my exclusive Imprint Access community. As Being part of this group gives you access to free CRI content, exclusive offers, discounts and more!

THE TRACK
THE KEY TO ENSURE SERVICE

DETERMINES
SUCCESS, RECOVERY & FORECASTING

THE DESTINATION

CUSTOMER RELATIONSHIP IMPRINTING
ELEMENT NUMBER SIX

THE TRACK DETERMINES THE DESTINATION

THE KEY TO ENSURING SERVICE SUCCESS, RECOVERING & FORECASTING

 CUSTOMER RELATIONSHIP IMPRINTING ELEMENT #6: STEER SERVICE WITH SYSTEMS

ROLLING DOWN THE TRACK

My father worked for the railroad my entire childhood. As a brakeman and conductor for Santa Fe Railroad, he worked on a train every day. When people asked what he did for a living, he often told them that he "moved the goods of America." It was hard work with long and varied hours.

One of the perks of having a dad who worked on the railroad is that he would sneak me onto the train to join him for work! This was totally against policy and likely illegal.

However, it was a dream come true for me as a young boy. Most little kids who have been on a train have only been a passenger on a novelty or amusement park train with a small track and a ride that lasts only a few minutes. I was now a real man, working on a real train, with my dad and real men...even though I was only 10 years old!

I remember the first time my mom snuck me onto the train to meet up with my dad. My dad picked me up and put me in the engine compartment with the engineer and my adventure began!

After we were moving along and gliding through the city on the rails, my dad set me in the engineer seat. For a brief time, as an elementary-age child, I was driving thousands of tons of locomotive steel! This was a huge step above most kids' experience of sitting on their parent's lap during a car ride.

I was driving a train, and it felt like we were going 100 M.P.H.

After a while, as we were quickly moving down the track, my dad said something that surprised me. He looked at me as I sat alone in the engineer's seat and said,

"MIKE, YOU'RE THE ENGINEER NOW."

For a moment, I was the one in charge of delivering the goods of America. As the new engineer, I surveyed my controls and pulled the loud train whistle to announce my new position to the cars we were passing.

I still remember some of the faces in the cars at the intersection when they saw a 10-year-old in the driver's seat. Their expressions were priceless. As a friendly new engineer, I waved to the stunned commuters. I am sure I was also smiling!

My dad then gave me what I thought was a very important instruction:

"TAKE THE WHEEL AND STEER US TO BARSTOW."

Alone in the engineer's seat, I began looking in front of me...high...low...but when I tried to find the steering wheel, I realized something very crucial:

THERE ARE NO STEERING WHEELS ON TRAINS!

Maybe you've never thought about it, but there is no need for a steering wheel on a train. No one aboard a train—not me, nor any other engineer—has ever steered it! The course taken by a locomotive is never determined by the engineer but by those who designed and laid the track.

THE TRACK DETERMINES THE DESTINATION!

The real engineer is not the one blowing the horn and sitting in the driver's seat; it's the one who created the course on which the train will ride.

THIS IS ALSO TRUE OF YOUR SERVICE.

It's up to the Service Architects to lay the service track so your employees can deliver consistent exceptional service and your customers can "steer" their experience on the track you create. This leads us to our final Customer Relationship Imprinting element.

CUSTOMER RELATIONSHIP IMPRINTING ELEMENT #6

STEER SERVICE WITH SYSTEMS

WHEN YOU CHOOSE TO LAY DOWN THE SERVICE TRACKS, YOU STEER BOTH YOUR SERVICE AND CUSTOMER RELATIONSHIPS.

Don't ever forget this:

WHOEVER LAYS THE TRACKS CONTROLS THE TRAIN!

This section is about providing systems for your employees to deliver consistent exceptional service, recover from a bad customer service experience, and forecast your customers' needs long before they know what they need...or want.

YOU NEED TO CREATE A SERVICE TRACK THAT GIVES YOUR CUSTOMER THE RIDE THEY DESIRE TO THE DESTINATION YOU DETERMINE.

Let me repeat that.

You need to create a service track that gives your customer the ride they desire to the destination you determine. Your customer should feel like they are steering the relationship! And although you want your customers to be in the driver's seat, "steering" the train, it is imperative that you create the track on which you want them to travel!

Laying down the service track will ensure a repeatable, measurable and trainable process.

Let's start with steering your service with the previously mentioned two factors: 1) Creating a service track that gives your customer the ride <u>they</u> desire and 2) laying down service tracks to the destination <u>you</u> determine.

#1 | STEER SERVICE WITH SYSTEMS BY GIVING YOUR CUSTOMERS THE RIDE THEY DESIRE.

CAPTURE, CATALOG & CONSTRUCT

Capture the data on customers, catalog and segment your customers, and construct the track that will give customers the desired experience to your determined destination.

Steering service with systems begins with capturing the data of your customers.

CAPTURE

You need to gather more information about your customer and begin to segment this information in order to understand the various types of customers you are reaching. You need to know who is boarding your service train.

CONSIDER CAPTURING FOUR TYPES OF CUSTOMER DATA.[29]

- **IDENTITY DATA:** The most basic information that identifies an individual (name, gender, age, phone number, address, email, social media handles, etc.).

- **DESCRIPTIVE DATA:** This is deeper data about your customer. You can get information such as their career aspirations, goals, etc., to help you see the types of customers you have.

- **BEHAVIORAL DATA:** This is the customer's social media habits, shopping preferences, what search words they are using to find you, as well the amount of time they spend online. You can use tools such as Google Analytics to help with this.

- **QUALITATIVE DATA:** Based on what you have discovered from the previous three types of data, this will help you determine how they really feel about your brand.

JOURNEY MAPPING YOUR CUSTOMER'S EXPERIENCE

Along with capturing the four types of data, you should create a customer journey map. This is the process of walking in your customer's shoes to help determine how they do business with you. There are multiple journey mapping books and digital resources available.

I will not spend time outlining the available resources, but I suggest you take a step, or deep dive, into the world of journey mapping to get a clearer picture of how to create your map.

As you look at the current experience, you will find important clues that will help you discover service deficiencies and unearth service opportunities that you did not previously see.

" YOU NEED TO CREATE A SERVICE TRACK THAT GIVES **YOUR CUSTOMERS** THE RIDE **THEY DESIRE** TO THE DESTINATION **YOU DETERMINE. "**

Michael Barnett

CUSTOMER RELATIONSHIP IMPRINTING

CATALOG

Finding data on your customers is the easy part. Making sure you have the right data—and that you can interpret it—is challenging. As you begin to look at all the data, you will start to build the various types of customers, or personas. Taking a part of data from one area and a piece of information from another portal or collection is an important part of cataloging your customer information in order to understand each customer type you are encountering. And then in the constructing step, you can create the right track for them.

CONSTRUCT

Using the captured data and cataloged customer types, you can now create various service tracks to give customers their desired experience based on their preferences, while creating a predetermined destination.

Steering service with systems will help to ensure the consistency that you are seeking. You will need to build in, or retrofit, measurability, repeatability and trainability. If you can't measure, repeat or train, then you do not have a system that will carry the weight of your service.

A few reminders to consider when constructing your service system:

- **Expectation** (What do you tell customers they can expect from their experience with you?)

- **Training** (Give employees the tools they need to deliver exceptional service.)

- **Monitoring** (You must monitor employee practices and your customers' experiences.)

- **Feedback** (Get from both customers and employees.)

- **Evaluation** (What is transpiring when your employees and customers interact?)

- **Communication** (Your customers should find it easy to reach you.)

- **Retrain & Reinforce** (Take all the above steps and use them for a retraining or reinforcing opportunity.)

- **Recovery Plans** (Do your employees know what to do, specifically, when something goes wrong?)

SERVICE GUIDES HELP YOUR STAFF DELIVER A CONSISTENT CUSTOMER EXPERIENCE. USING A CRM SYSTEM MAKES THIS PROCESS A LOT EASIER TO REPEAT, MEASURE AND TRAIN.

#2 | STEER SERVICE WITH SYSTEMS BY LAYING DOWN SERVICE TRACKS TO THE DESTINATION YOU DETERMINE.

LET'S LOOK AT HOW A SERVICE GUIDE CAN HELP YOUR STAFF.

Here are two fictitious day spas:

Refresh Day Spa & *Ohana Day Spa*.

Let's see the difference when there's no system in place at Refresh Day Spa. Then we will look at Ohana, which has a system in place to help deliver exceptional service.

REFRESH DAY SPA
CUSTOMER EXPERIENCE WITHOUT A GUIDE IN PLACE

Customer walks into the reception area.

Receptionist: "I'll be with you in a minute."

Customer is standing there waiting for the receptionist to be ready or finished with her task.

Receptionist: "Hello. How can I help you?"

Customer: "I have a 2:00 pm appointment for a facial."

R: "What's your name?"

C: "My name is Sally Hansen."

R: "Who is your appointment with?"

C: "I'm not totally sure. It's my first time here, and the guy on the phone didn't tell me when I set the appointment."

R: "Okay, looks like they are working you in, so either Jasmine or Steven will be with you in a little bit. That will be eighty-five dollars—cash, credit, debit or Apple pay?"

C: "Debit."

R: "Swipe your card. Okay...you can take a seat over there *(pointing to the lounge)*, and we will let you know when we are ready for you."

On the surface, there's likely not a lot that stands out as bad customer service at Refresh Day Spa—mostly because it's *not* a bad customer experience; it's just not exceptional service.

How could this experience look with a service system in place? Notice the personalization and detail that gets covered in the brief transaction at Ohana Day Spa.

After this, you will see what some of the systems are that were used to provide a higher level of service. None of the receptionist's interactions are accidental.

OHANA DAY SPA
CUSTOMER EXPERIENCE WITH A SERVICE GUIDE IN PLACE

Customer walks towards the reception area.

Receptionist: *(Before customer reaches the receptionist)* "Hello, Miss Hansen. Welcome. We've been looking forward to seeing you today. My name is Sara. How are you doing today? I love that top you're wearing...so cute!"

C: "Thank you. I just got it."

R: "Jasmine is on her way up, and it looks like you used our online payment option so you are all set, Miss Hansen."

C: "Great. Should I sit in the lounge?"

R: "You can, but since it's your first time here, before your facial, if you have 15 extra minutes, I can have Jasmine also give you a complimentary mini-microdermabrasion treatment today."

C: "Thank you so much, but I have to pick up my kids after school today, so I don't have time."

R: "No problem. I am going to give you this pass for the next time you come in, and it's good for the free mini-micro when you have more time." *She hands her the pass after she personally signs it.*

C: "Wow...thanks. That's so nice."

R: "What grade are your kids in? I just have one, but she's in half-day kindergarten, so I pick her up early."

C: "I have one in first grade and one in third. They're a handful."

R: "All the more reason to take a little time for yourself. I'm glad you came in today. Jasmine is great...here she is now. Have a great session, and I am here if you need anything else."

R: "Jasmine, take care of my new friend. She's a mom who deserves some special treatment!"

C: "Thank you. You've already made my day!"

Okay, this is a little over the top, but you get the idea.

TAKE A MINUTE AND REALLY COMPARE THESE TWO EXPERIENCES.

SOME GLARING DIFFERENCES

Refresh: Waited for the customer to make first contact and made her wait.
Ohana: Was ready for the interaction and knew the name of the customer even though it was her first time at the spa.

Refresh: Asked the customer what services she was getting done and by whom.
Ohana: Communicated that she knew the services the customer was getting done and who would be giving the treatment.

Refresh: Overshared that she was just a work-in. Talk about not feeling like a special customer!

Ohana: Offered a "surprise" complimentary service and made the extra effort to sign the pass, as it can give more perceived legitimacy or at least personalization.

Refresh: Overall, there was no personalization. The receptionist was focused on the transaction, not the customer. No one would walk away from this encounter feeling appreciated.

Ohana: Overall, there was attention to the details of the transaction, but the focus was on the customer—knowing her name, being complimentary and engaging. It didn't hurt that she also was given a free service.

The owners train this way because they know that the more time customers spend in their spa, the more opportunity the staff have to make their day.

LET'S LOOK AT THE SERVICE GUIDE PUT IN PLACE TO STEER OHANA DAY SPA'S SERVICE.

HERE IS A BRIEF SYNOPSIS OF THE SERVICE GUIDE THAT IS IN PLACE FOR RECEPTIONISTS WHO WORK AT OHANA DAY SPA.

"Find a way to make our customer's day" by:

- Looking at your list of appointments and looking at the customer photo, if one is uploaded to our site.
- Looking at your computer and, as you recognize the customer, greeting them by name, making eye contact, and smiling.
- Complimenting their personality, beauty, attire, or attitude.
- Finding out what makes this customer **S.M.I.L.E.**

  S: Social connections? (Are they married? Do they have friends? Kids?)

  M: Mad—what upsets them?

  I: Interests? (What do they like to do?)

L: Living? (What do they do for a living?)

E: Extra activities to list? (Notate them in your CRM software.)

- Look in our computer system to determine any details that have been inputted about the services they've previously received as well as any issues and preferences. If a new customer, import the new data from what they set up on our site. (This is a short but important form that tells the spa a little more info about Miss Hansen and will be added to each time she receives services.)

- Offer them a free service of any kind they have not experienced with us before. Or you can upgrade a service they are currently using at a 20% discount.

- After their session, ask, "We love having you here. Is there anything special I can do for you before you go?" This is an engaging question that communicates we want to do more for the customer, rather than just saying, "Thanks. See you next time."

- If they are a first-time customer, offer them a related free service to the service they are getting today—up to a $45 value.

OHANA DAY SPA'S CUSTOMERS ARE GETTING THE RIDE THEY DESIRE TO THE DESTINATION THAT OHANA DETERMINED.

#3 | STEER SERVICE WITH SYSTEMS BY USING SERVICE SCRIPTS AND LEAD SHEETS.

My oldest daughter is a musician. She spends her days performing, leading worship, writing songs and creating music guides called "lead sheets" for other musicians so they can play together. When it comes to playing a predetermined piece of music, there are a couple of ways to read it. The two most typical types of musical notations that musicians use to play a song are sheet music and lead sheets.

WHAT'S THE DIFFERENCE BETWEEN SHEET MUSIC AND LEAD SHEETS?

"The main difference between lead sheets and sheet music is that sheet music notates every single note. Lead sheets, on the other hand, notate the melody on the staff, but leave it up to the musician to interpret the chords."[30]

WHY DOES THIS MATTER TO YOUR SERVICE?

You also have a few options when it comes to your employees' customer service talk-tracks. You can choose a service script (like sheet music), where you give your staff a script to follow word for word. Or you can give them a lead sheet, which gives them the freedom to communicate your established principles by using some of their own language.

There is a place for both options. The upside of a script is you get the same answer from every employee. This is also the downside. Your staff could come off like script-reading robots.

Lead sheets also have an upside: they allow your employees to use their personal communication style and verbiage, and like the script, it is also the downside. You would be trusting that your staff know how to communicate professionally.

Most businesses have a mix of both styles. But it's important that your staff understand when to use scripts and when they can use lead sheets.

#4 | STEER SERVICE WITH SYSTEMS BY PLANNING FOR RECOVERY.

Your service will fail every day. Let me say this differently: everyone's service fails every day. Service defects are inevitable. It is the reality of being human. However, when you have the right recovery strategy in place, you have an opportunity to impress a customer whom you just disappointed. The important service opportunity for Service Architects is to build into your system the plan for what to do when you have come up short on delivering exceptional service.

HERE ARE A FEW THINGS FOR YOUR STAFF TO CONSIDER WHEN DEALING WITH A SERVICE ERROR:

1. **BE PREPARED FOR ERRORS.** Progress, not perfection, should guide your service. Go through the data that you have collected, your journey mapping as well as service guides and find deficiencies. Create a plan for recovering from these issues.

2. **ADDRESS VULNERABLE AREAS.** Look where service defects are most likely to exist and fix them before issues arise. Do you need to change some policies or procedures to anticipate reoccurring issues? Being proactive prevents many problems.

3. **USE THE INTERNAL SERVICE SWITCH TRIGGERS.** Guide your staff to be customer-centric when speaking with customers by using the I.S.S. Triggers. Do you want your staff to prove they're right (even if they are) or look for ways to make your customer's day, even if it means swallowing some pride? Humility and a desire to serve go a long way!

4. **ALWAYS CONSIDER THE CLV.** The Customer Lifetime Value should be at the forefront of your employees' minds when dealing with an issue. Do you really want to lose a customer who will bring you thousands of dollars in income over their lifetime of business with you over a small policy, an extra charge, or an expired coupon? Choose your battles.

INSPECT WHAT YOU EXPECT.

For service recovery to have the greatest impact, you need to have someone in each department/category of business/location/etc. be responsible for the customer service efforts. You must inspect what you expect and provide rewards and accountability for these efforts. Just as people in your company check the financials hourly, daily, year to date, etc., so too do you need to have a schedule to inspect what you're expecting.

Creating realistic goals and tiered expectations is part of great service. Think of these as road signs for your employees. They need to see the forward motion of their efforts as they are taking customers on the track of customer service.

If your staff don't have signs, or goals, to help keep them interested, then they will lose interest or simply not know the expectations.

#5 | STEER SERVICE WITH SYSTEMS THROUGH SMART SERVICE FORECASTING.

WHAT'S SMART SERVICE FORECASTING?

Steering your service with systems not only means giving your customers the ride they desire; it also means that you need a system that's able to predict the next need before it arises.

Anticipating what your customers need and laying down track by using the system you have in place is what Smart Service Forecasting is all about.

A SMALL NATURAL FOODS GROCERY CHAIN USED SMART SERVICE FORECASTING TO TAKE THE LEAD DURING THE PANDEMIC.

When the COVID-19 pandemic hit hard in March 2020, supermarkets were battlegrounds.

Do you remember the TV images—or maybe you experienced it yourself—where people were clearing the shelves and fighting over toilet paper and water?

Imagine having a disability or being elderly and being unable to stand in line for a long period of time. Did you ever think about how these people would be getting all their food and supplies? One small grocery chain did.

Clark's Nutrition, a Southern California chain of four natural foods stores, was the first in the country to offer special shopping hours for elderly and disabled customers during this time. They made these choices before the largest grocery chains in the country even knew what to do.

This is Smart Service Forecasting!

What were the results for this grocery chain?

HAVING THE FORESIGHT TO SEE THE NEED BEFORE ANYONE ELSE RESULTED IN VIRAL POSTS OF CUSTOMERS SINGING THE PRAISES OF THIS COMPANY LIKE THEY'VE NEVER SEEN IN THE PREVIOUS 48 YEARS OF BUSINESS!

They received praise and posts from as far as Louisiana!

MORE IMPORTANTLY, THEY SAW A TIDAL WAVE OF CUSTOMER ATTRACTION, ACQUISITION AND RETENTION.

New customers were drawn to the stores. Even if they didn't fit the elderly or disabled criteria, people were attracted to the four locations. There was a huge increase in customer acquisition—in part due to the availability of water and toilet paper! But many of these customers discovered a store that they had never even considered prior to the crisis and made multiple purchases.

The retention of both these new customers and regular customers was greatly boosted. Prior to the crisis, Clark's had a Net Promoter Score (NPS) of 58. The NPS is the standardized metric used to measure customer satisfaction. This score of 58 is good for this industry. After the pandemic, their score was 68, which is great!

WHY?

Because people remember whom they can trust after a trial of this magnitude. Just ask any military veteran who has been in battle, and they will tell you that you'll remember who had your back in the foxhole...and who didn't!

SERVING CUSTOMERS WHERE YOU RECOGNIZE THEIR NEED BEFORE THEY DO IS THE HOLY GRAIL OF CUSTOMER SERVICE.

A good plan should always involve mechanisms to recognize these unseen opportunities. What is something that your team is doing now that was an early response to what your customers didn't know they needed until you provided it? Smart Service Forecasting should be an integral part of your service system.

You can look at data to determine the future, have service contingency plans, as well as keep your staff enlisted to recognize needed patterns to help with your Smart Service Forecasting.

It is also crucial to provide your team with a communication avenue to help you capture, catalog and construct the systems that will help you steer your service more effectively!

ALL SYSTEMS "GO"!

Giving your customers the ride they desire by laying down service tracks to the destination you desire is the beginning of systematizing your service. As you use scripts, lead sheets, make plans for recovery and add Smart Service Forecasting to your service system, your consistency will increase.

STEERING WITH SYSTEMS INVOLVES MORE OF YOUR STAFF THAN ANY OF THE OTHER CRI ELEMENTS.
DEVELOPING YOUR SYSTEMS IS AN ONGOING PROCESS.

It will require a Service Architect leading the charge and creating or retrofitting your system to make service the primary focus of your business.

> **" SERVING CUSTOMERS WHERE YOU RECOGNIZE THEIR NEED BEFORE THEY DO IS THE HOLY GRAIL OF CUSTOMER SERVICE. "**

Michael Barnett

CUSTOMER RELATIONSHIP IMPRINTING

SECTION SIX:
PRACTICAL APPLICATION

STEER SERVICE
WITH SYSTEMS

CRI LEXICON
Key words or phrases from this section

"STEER SERVICE WITH SYSTEMS" - "WHOEVER LAYS THE TRACKS CONTROLS THE TRAIN" - SERVICE GUIDES - SERVICE SCRIPTS & LEAD SHEETS - SMART SERVICE FORECASTING

PRACTICAL IMPRESSIONS
Practical questions & exercises from this section for personal application

#1 WHAT ARE 2 CONSISTENT COMPLIMENTS/COMPLAINTS ABOUT YOUR SERVICE? IS THERE A SYSTEM THAT NEEDS TO BE EXAMINED TO INCREASE THE COMPLIMENTED AREAS & DECREASE THE CRITICIZED AREAS?

Go to: SixSidedService.com for 9 more questions/exercises from section six.

GROUP THERAPY SESSION
For group reading, team building and group discussion

#1 AS A GROUP, DESCRIBE YOUR SERVICE TRACKS THAT GIVE YOUR CUSTOMER THE RIDE THEY DESIRE. DISCUSS CURRENT & FUTURE DESTINATIONS YOUR COMPANY HAS DETERMINED TO TAKE THEM WITH YOUR SERVICE.

Go to: SixSidedService.com for 9 more group questions/exercises from section six.

IMPRINT ACCESS
Get more imprinting tools & exclusive content

Text me directly at: **949.577.8397** and I will not only respond to you, but you'll become a part of my exclusive Imprint Access community. Being part of this group gives you access to free CRI content, exclusive offers, discounts and more!

FINAL
IMPRESSIONS

CUSTOMER RELATIONSHIP IMPRINTING
CONCLUSION

FINAL IMPRESSIONS

It takes guts to put your customer at the forefront of your business decisions. It also takes a strategy and a commitment to a strong service path. I have tried to outline within each section of *Customer Relationship Imprinting* a clear understanding of each CRI element so your organization can deliver exceptional service as you achieve Customer Relationship Imprinting with every customer you encounter.

I hope the various parts of this book will live in your staff's service lexicon and be heard within your corporate meetings, department phone calls, as well as frontline workroom floors. May phrases like "Relational Velcro," "the Internal Service Switch," "Kindness is currency," and other ideas to which you've been exposed find their way through your organization—and ultimately to the benefit of your customers.

Another wish I have for you is that *Customer Relationship Imprinting* won't be just another service book to add to your library, but that it would be a calling for you to execute these 6 elements day in and day out. I hope that as a Service Architect, you take these tools and build something amazing.

SOME READERS WILL GET TO THE END OF THIS BOOK AND SAY, "THERE'S A LOT MORE TO CUSTOMER SERVICE THAN THIS."

THEY WILL BE RIGHT.

I hope that every Service Architect who reads this will choose to add to this necessary framework outlined in *Customer Relationship Imprinting*. It's also a reminder that service will always be morphing and growing, just as customer experience will inevitably change.

But for a minute, just imagine if you started to find a way to make your customer's day, enlist and empower Service Architects, develop customer-centric employees, treat brand and service as inseparable, nurture your culture and steer your service with systems! If you can execute these 6 elements, you will be miles ahead of your competitors!

Although you are getting ready to close this book, I want to keep our relationship open. Text me directly at 949.577.8397 or email me at michael@sixsidedservice.com.

I WILL ALSO CONTINUE TO PROVIDE FREE CONTENT TO MY TEXTING COMMUNITY THROUGH IMPRINT ACCESS.

Customer Relationship Imprinting is yours for the taking.

I look forward to hearing how your team is

"ATTRACTING, ACQUIRING, AND RETAINING MORE CUSTOMERS WHO WILL FOLLOW YOU REGARDLESS OF CIRCUMSTANCES"!

Let me close our time together the same way I began it:

May the touch of Customer Relationship Imprinting activate and connect your customer service in a whole new way!

PHOTOCOPY THE FOLLOWING PAGE AND PLACE IT WHERE YOU CAN SEE IT EVERY DAY

CUSTOMER RELATIONSHIP IMPRINTING

"THE ABILITY TO ATTRACT, ACQUIRE, AND RETAIN MORE CUSTOMERS WHO WILL FOLLOW YOU REGARDLESS OF CIRCUMSTANCES!"

THE 6 ELEMENTS THAT ENSURE EXCEPTIONAL SERVICE WITHOUT EXCEPTION

 FIND A WAY TO MAKE THEIR DAY

 ENLIST & EMPOWER SERVICE ARCHITECTS

 DEVELOP CUSTOMER-CENTRIC EMPLOYEES

 TREAT BRAND & SERVICE AS INSEPARABLE

 NURTURE THE CULTURE

 STEER SERVICE WITH SYSTEMS

NOTES

1. Craig McVoy, "80% of CEOs Believe They Deliver Superior Customer Experience…" *Medium*, May 6, 2016, https://medium.com/@CMcVoy/80-of -ceos-believe-they-deliver-superior-customer-experience-661efabd16b0.

2. Vala Afashar, "50 Important Customer Experience Stats for Business Leaders," *Huffpost*, last updated on December 6, 2017, https://www.huffpost.com/ entry/50-important-customer-exp_b_8295772.

3. "70% of Buying Experiences Are Based on How the Customer Feels They Are Being Treated," *Industry Analysts*, December 4, 2017, https://www .industryanalysts.com/12417_greatamerica//.

4. Dimensional Research, "Customer Service and Business Results: A Survey of Customer Service from Mid-Size Companies," Dimensional Research, April 2013, https://d16cvnquvjw7pr.cloudfront.net/resources/whitepapers/Zendesk_ WP_Customer_Service_and_Business_Results.pdf.

5. "RightNow's Annual Research Shows 86 Percent of U.S. Adults Will Pay More for a Better Customer Experience," *BusinessWire*, January 11, 2012, https://www .businesswire.com/news/home/20120111005284/en/RightNow%E2%80%99s -Annual-Research-Shows-86-Percent-of-U.S.-Adults-Will-Pay-More-For-A -Better-Customer-Experience.

6. "#WellActually, Americans Say Customer Service is Better Than Ever," *American Express*, December 15, 2017, https://about.americanexpress.com/all-news/news -details/2017/WellActually-Americans-Say-Customer-Service-is-Better-Than -Ever/default.aspx.

7. "Enlist," *Merriam-Webster*, https://www.merriam-webster.com/dictionary/enlist.

8. "Reticular Activating System," *Oxford Reference*, https://www.oxfordreference. com/view/10.1093/oi/authority.20110803100416605.

9. Tobias van Schneider, "If You Want It, You Might Get It. The Reticular Activating System Explained," *Medium*, June 22, 2017, https://medium.com/ desk-of-van-schneider/if-you-want-it-you-might-get-it-the-reticular-activating -system-explained-761b6ac14e53.

10. Judy Willis, "Obtaining & Sustaining The Brain's Attentive Focus," November 4, 2013, https://cdn.ymaws.com/www.aimsmddc.org/resource/resmgr/imported/ WillisJudyHandoutPM-4.doc.

11. Kursat Ozenc quoted in Stephen Hampshire, "Rituals for Work," *TLF Research*, accessed October 12, 2021, https://www.tlfresearch.com/rituals-for-work/.

12. Moira Vetter, "The $40,000 Olive: How Entrepreneurs Can Spend Time Saving Money," *Forbes*, June 4, 2015, https://www.forbes.com/sites/moiravetter/2015/06/04/the-40000-olive-how-entrepreneurs-can-spend-time-saving-money/.

13. Jason Aten, "A Customer Discovered Their $350 Lego Set Was Missing Pieces. The Company's Response Was Brilliant," *Inc.com*, accessed October 13, 2021, inc.com/jason-aten/a-customer-discovered-their-350-lego-set-was-missing-pieces-companys-response-was-brilliant.html.

14. Robert Wollan et al., "Put Your Trust in Hyper-Relevance," Accenture, 2017, 4, https://www.accenture.com/t20180219T081429Z__w__/us-en/_acnmedia/PDF-71/Accenture-Global-DD-GCPR-Hyper-Relevance-POV-V12.pdf#zoom=50.

15. Blake Morgan, "100 of the Most Customer-Centric Companies," *Forbes*, June 30, 2019, https://www.forbes.com/sites/blakemorgan/2019/06/30/100-of-the-most-customer-centric-companies/.

16. David M. Flanagan, *Rudder: Strategic Brand Clarity*, 2nd ed. (Sacramento, CA: S-Club Publishing, 2018), 18.

17. Nike, "Breaking Barriers," Nike.com, https://purpose.nike.com/#:~:text=Nike%20exists%20to%20bring%20inspiration,body%2C%20you%20are%20an%20athlete.

18. Alex Abad-Santos, "Nike's Colin Kaepernick Ad Sparked a Boycott—and Earned $6 Billion for Nike," *Vox*, September 24, 2018, https://www.vox.com/2018/9/24/17895704/nike-colin-kaepernick-boycott-6-billion.

19. David Goran, "Testing the First Bulletproof Vests—There Were Men Who Took Turns Shooting Each Other," February 23, 2016, https://www.thevintagenews.com/2016/02/23/dangerous-job-testing-bulletproof-vests/.

20. Carolyn Crafts, "Broken Promises: When Brands Don't Deliver What They Promise," April 1, 2019, https://www.fullsurge.com/blog/broken-promises-when-brands-dont-live-up-to-what-they-promised-to-deliver.

21. Linda Gerchick, "Broken Promises: When a Brand Fails to Deliver on Its Commitments," n.d., https://justsoldit.com/broken-promises-when-a-brand-fails-to-deliver-on-its-commitments/.

22. Iftekharuddin Choudhury, "Culture," Texas A&M University, accessed October 13, 2021, http://people.tamu.edu/~i-choudhury/culture.html.

23. Rose Leadem, "10 Extreme Career Changes by Celebrities," *Houston Chronicle*, February 26, 2017, https://www.chron.com/news/article/10-Extreme-Career -Changes-by-Celebrities-10958869.php.

24. Ibid.

25. Ethan Trex, "Strange Early Jobs of 23 Famous People," CNN.com, accessed October 15, 2021, https://www.cnn.com/2009/LIVING/worklife/05/29/ mf.how.celebs.got.start/index.html.

26. Ibid.

27. Ibid.

28. "30 Awful Jobs Celebrities Had Before They Became Famous," *BestLifeOnline. com*, June 1, 2018, https://bestlifeonline.com/30-awful-jobs-celebrities-had -before-they-became-famous/.

29. Rob Fitzgerald, "4 Types of Customer Data to Enhance Your Marketing Campaigns," *Connext Digital*, June 20, 2019, https://connextdigital.com/types -customer-data-enhance-marketing-campaigns-infographic/.

30. Julian Harnish, "Lead Sheets vs Chord Charts vs Sheet Music vs Tabs," *Find Your Melody*, February 8, 2021, https://findyourmelody.com/lead-sheets-vs-chord -charts-vs-sheet-music-vs-tabs/.

"LET'S WORK TOGETHER"

Michael Barnett

michael@sixsidedservice.com

Michael Barnett is the Chief Service Architect, lead trainer, and president of Six-Sided Service. After two decades of developing brands and working in the advertising space, Michael noticed brands were continually being negatively impacted by failed advertising campaigns that fell flat due to one thing...marginal customer service. This began a new quest to determine how these service deficiencies could be inspected, identified and corrected. Customer Relationship Imprinting was birthed out of Michael's desire to help businesses move from 'acceptable' service to exceptional service.

Michael is transforming the customer service landscape through his exclusive Six-Sided Service formula and Customer Relationship Imprinting system. His ability to help companies attract, acquire and retain more customers through the Customer Relationship Imprinting courses, speaking engagements, and training tools is enabling Michael to have a positive imprint on businesses of all sizes.

Michael lives in Southern California and can often be found enjoying the beach, great food, and music with his wife, Brenda, and two daughters, Roxie and Cheyenne.

SIXSIDEDSERVICE.COM